SKY SPORTS

SKY SPORTS

CONTENTS

Edited by: **DAVE SMITH**
Designed by: **STEVE McGARRY**

Published by

Pedigree®
BOOKS

under licence from British Sky Broadcasting

PEDIGREE BOOKS Ltd
The Old Rectory
Matford Lane
Exeter
Devon EX2 4PS
©1999
Tm & © BSKYB Ltd. 1999
SKY SPORTS is a Trademark of BSKYB

£6.99
SSI

WELCOME!
TO THE FIRST-EVER
SKY SPORTS
SPORTING ANNUAL

In the past year Sky Sports has broadcast an incredible 25,000 hours of sport. We have shown more than 250 live football matches, 120 days of live cricket, 100 live golf tournaments, 80 rugby union matches and added sports like speedway and greyhounds to our ever expanding line-up.

There have been so many live events, so many different sports, from across the world. But certain images are still vivid, made immortal by television.

The climax to the 1998-99 football season will remain long in my memory. The Premiership was decided on the very last day; and the enduring images are of United fans shocked as Spurs took the lead, then Arsenal fans stunned as the final result filtered back from Old Trafford to Highbury.

The other side of Manchester had cause for celebration too when the Nationwide Play-Off Finals produced another dramatic result. Manchester City came from behind in injury time, drew level in extra time, then won promotion, on penalties, to the First Division.

Then Graham Taylor's Watford rose to the Premiership when their victory at Wembley - watched live in Seattle by chairman Elton John - secured promotion for the second season running.

International football, too, had its drama: Glenn Hoddle departed, Howard Wilkinson lead England against World Cup-winning France, then Kevin Keegan's reign started in style with a Paul Scholes hat-trick at Wembley. But, for me three other goals really stand out - Ryan Giggs' amazing solo run against Arsenal in the FA Cup, Player of the Year David Ginola with a similar stunning Cup goal against Barnsley, and a 15-year old girl, Alexia Hunn, who took on six Scottish players to score one of the best goals ever seen under Wembley's famous twin towers.

Cricket took centre-stage in May and June with the World Cup back in England for the first time in 16 years. The home side may have left the party before the Super Six stage, but that made us all look more closely at the amazing overseas talents - such as Shoaib Akhtar and Lance Klusener - and it certainly did not subdue the legions of international fans - they made it a true carnival of cricket at the grounds.

One British success story, Colin Montgomerie, secured his sixth Order of Merit in 1998 and will hope to pick up another Ryder Cup medal in September this year. In between golfers have played too many impossible shots, too many awesome drives to mention. But one Major, the US Open, stands out for sheer drama; the title won by Payne Stewart on the last stroke of the final match - and the personal drama of his opponent Phil Mickelson with pager in pocket, prepared to walk away from the tournament - at any stage - to join his wife for the arrival of their first child.

There were so many more magic moments I can clearly recall - new cap Alex Tudor scoring 99 N.O to take new captain Nasser Hussain to victory in this summer's first Test, the nail-bighting climax to South Africa vs Australia in the Cricket World Cup, England's gritty draw with rugby's All Blacks to prevent their opponents setting a new world record of consecutive wins - and all have one thing in common: they were live on Sky Sports.

In the ten years since Sky Television was launched we have been privileged to see some marvelous entertainment - we are grateful to the players, the coaches, the teams and the fans who have made it. For our part we have launched five sports channels - Sky Sports 1, Sky Sports 2, Sky Sports 3, Sky Sports News and now Sky Sports Extra and pioneered some new TV techniques. We hope our coverage, our camera work and our reporting has matched their achievements.

With this new Sky Sports annual, the aim is the same - to provide great value, sound information and excellent entertainment.

I hope you enjoy it.

Vic Wakeling
Head of Sport

WIN!

10 SKY SPORTS VIDEOS!

PLUS! 20 Sky Sports T-shirts to give away

The race for the 1998-99 Football Premiership title was one of the most exciting for years and, of course, all of the action was brilliantly captured on Sky Sports. Now the best of the entertainment and drama has been put together on one breathtaking video – 'The Battle for the FA Carling Premiership'- and we have got 10 copies to give away in our opening competition.

All you have to do to stand a chance of winning one of these great videos is simply write and tell us your own personal highlight of the 1998-99 Premiership season. The first ten original and interesting suggestions will receive a copy of the video, while 20 other runners-up will get an exclusive Sky Sports T-shirt.

Send your suggestions to:
**Sky Sports Annual 'Video' Competition,
Pedigree Books,
The Old Rectory,
Matford Lane,
Exeter EX2 4PS**

Closing date for entries is February 28, 2000.

Battle for the FA Carling Premiership 98/99

Sky Sports' official review of the 1998/99 F.A. Carling Premiership

'Battle for the FA Carling Premiership'

COMING UP NEXT:

WE BEGIN OUR ANNUAL IN THE BOXING RING AND PAY TRIBUTE TO TWO GREAT BRITISH CHAMPIONS, LENNOX LEWIS AND PRINCE NASEEM HAMED.

SKY PRESENTER PAUL DEMPSEY

BOXING REVIEW

It has been another fantastic year of boxing full of drama, controversy, skill and the customary dosage of sheer bravery and dedication by so many wonderful fighters at all weights. And Skys' expert boxing presenter Paul Dempsey has never been far away from the action. Pride of place, as far as the British contingent is concerned at least, goes to Lennox Lewis and Prince Naseem Hamed whose performances in '99 made compelling viewing for those of you who tuned into Sky Box office to witness some magnificent, value-for-money entertainment. And when it comes to entertaining few do it better than Prince Naz who, at the time of this publication going to press, was still unbeaten and still dazzling opponents with his mastery of the ring, and unique array of boxing skills which stand him apart from anyone in the world. There's certainly never a dull moment when the Prince is around and the same could also be said of fellow Brit Lennox Lewis who continued to enhance his reputation whilst, at the same time, persuading cynical American boxing fans that he had earned the right to be classed among the best. Who could forget his sensational scrap with Evander Holyfield; and the controversy which followed. Make up your own mind about the outcome of the tied verdict. As far as Paul is concerned, however, and no doubt many fight fans would agree, his fight of the year was the first contest for the World Cruiserweight title between the irrepressible Chris Eubank and Carl Thompson. A memorable and intriguing tussle in every sense. Oscar de la Hoya gets Paul's vote as the outstanding individual of the year while, closer to home, the ever-emerging talent of Julius Frances gets the nod as the most improved fighter of the year. All in all, a magnificent year of boxing; with the guarantee of more thrills and spills to come in the New Year.

SKY

box office

PRINCE NASEEM – "his fights are always thrilling ..."

BEST FIGHT OF '99: CARL THOMPSON v CHRIS EUBANK
World Cruiserweight title (1st fight)
BEST INDIVIDUAL PERFORMANCE: OSCAR DE LA HOYA
for expanding his reputation and considerable wealth with his two
WBC Welterweight victories over **IKE QUARTEY** in February
and **OBA CARR** in May.
BEST HEAVYWEIGHT IN THE WORLD: LENNOX LEWIS
BEST OTHER FIGHTER: PRINCE NASEEM
because his fights are always thrilling, especially the classic
confrontation with **KEVIN KELLY**
MOST IMPROVED FIGHTER: JULIUS FRANCES
MOST DISAPPOINTING PERFORMANCE:
IKE QUARTEY v OSCAR DE LA HOYA
as **QUARTEY** failed to deliver on any of his promises in that fight, and
failed to seize the opportunity presented to him

LENNOX LEWIS – "the best Heavyweight in the world ..."

THE SKY SPORTS JURY

PAUL didn't make it onto the *SKY JURY* in our *SKYSPORTS* soccer annual, but he is a big football fan so here are his men and moments of the year:

1 PLAYER OF THE SEASON
DAVID BECKHAM (Manchester United)
I am astonished he did not receive either the PFA or Football Writers' awards

2 MANAGER OF THE SEASON
PAUL JEWELL (Bradford)
Achieved promotion from the First Division playing constantly attractive football

3 TEAM OF THE SEASON
CHELTENHAM TOWN
I won't nominate the obvious ... instead I will welcome Cheltenham Town to the Football League

4 GAME OF THE SEASON
PRESTON v ARSENAL
The Preston v Arsenal FA Cup tie because it proved the essence, romance and passion of the FA Cup lives on

5 GOAL OF THE SEASON
Any of **DAVID BECKHAM'S** special free kicks

6 SAVE OF THE SEASON
So many but the **overall impact of MAGNUS** HEDMAN at COVENTRY made him my goalkeeper of the season

7 GOOF OF THE SEASON
Not rewarding PETER TAYLOR for his outstanding service with the ENGLAND UNDER-21 team

8 BUY OF THE SEASON
TOTTENHAM HOTSPUR getting GEORGE GRAHAM as their manager - whatever the cost!

9 SURPRISE OF THE SEASON
That MARCEL DESAILLY was unable to galvanise CHELSEA'S defence to enable this talented side to win the title

10 OUTSTANDING MOMENT OF THE SEASON
DAVID GINOLA'S goal for SPURS against BARNSLEY in the FA Cup

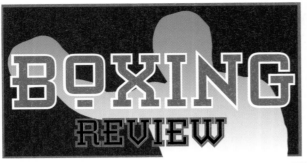

BOXING REVIEW

As we all know, Prince Naseem Hamed is no shrinking violet when it comes to talking about himself, his ability and his supreme confidence in and out of the ring. But it was a series of statements made by an opponent – Billy Hardy – which made compelling reading and gave a telling insight into what it's like being on the receiving end of a Prince pounding. Hardy was speaking from painful experience after suffering the indignity of a technical knockout in the first round of his challenge for Naz's IBF and WBO Featherweight titles in May, 1997.

No hiding from the facts, Hardy was honest in his assessment of the most natural boxing talent this country has ever produced…

"Naz has immense power in both hands. With the first shot he hit with me on that night I felt my nose crack and my mouth go numb. I was the number one challenger but he wiped me away. I honestly believe he's got something special in his hands."

Needless to say, the Prince was in no mood to disagree with his opponent and, on one occasion, went as far as to say: "In my eyes, nothing can stop me from becoming a legend."

PRINCE BORN TO BE A KING!

NAZ STATS

Birthplace: **Sheffield**
Date of birth: **February 12, 1974**
Height: **5ft 3ins**
Fighting weight: **122-126lbs**
Chest: **36 ins**   *Reach:* **63 ins**
Waist: **29 ins**   *Thigh:* **29ins**
Fist: **10ins**

Here are a few more priceless **PRINCE** statements – all delivered with customary modesty…

I DON'T JUST HAVE PUNCHING POWER. I HAVE ACCURACY, SPEED, TIMING…EVERYTHING. I'M PROBABLY THE HARDEST-PUNCHING FEATHERWEIGHT EVER!

THERE IS MORE TO COME FROM ME YET BUT I'LL JUST KEEP WINNING EVERYTHING AND RETIRE UNDEFEATED. I DON'T THINK ANYONE CAN BEAT ME!

I WANT TO EARN ENOUGH MONEY SO I CAN BUY OIL RIGS. SO I CAN SCATTER IT ABOUT, GIVE IT TO FRIENDS AND FAMILY!

I WOULDN'T SAY I'M EVIL AND I DON'T GO OUT WITH THE INTENTION OF PUTTING ANYONE IN HOSPITAL. THE TRUTH IS I HAVE NO FEAR AND I WILL FACE ANYONE OR ANYTHING !

I DON'T CARE WHO I FIGHT. I'M REALLY NOT BOTHERED. THE RESULT WILL ALWAYS BE THE SAME. IF I HIT A MAN ON THE CHIN, HE'S GOING TO GET KNOCKED OUT – NO QUESTION !

SKY box office

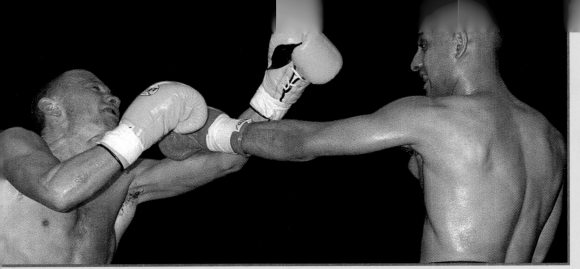

"NOTHING CAN STOP ME BECOMING A LEGEND ..."

BOXING REVIEW

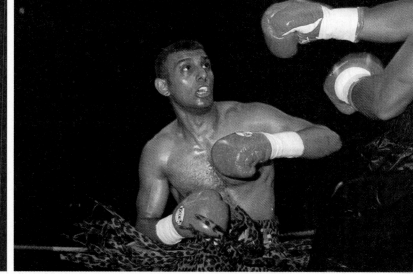

PRINCE'S FIGHT PATH TO GREATNESS !

At the time of this publication going to press, PRINCE NASEEM had won all 32 of his professional fights, 29 of them inside the distance. Here's how:-

1992
April 14	v RICKY BEARD	Mansfield	KO 2nd
April 25	v SHAUN NORMAN	Manchester	TKO 2nd
May 23	v ANDREW BLOOMER	Birmingham	TKO 2nd
July 14	v MIGUEL MATTHEWS	Mayfair	TKO 3rd
October 7	v DES GARGANO	Sunderland	TKO 4th
November 12	v PETER BUCKLEY	Liverpool	Points

1993
February 24	v ALAN LEY	Wembley	KO 2nd
May 26	v KEVIN JENKINS	Mansfield	TKO 3rd
September 24	v CHRIS CLARKSON	Dublin	KO 2nd

1994
January 29	v PETER BUCKLEY	Cardiff	TKO 4th
April 9	v JOHN MICELI	Mansfield	KO 1st
May 11	v VICENZO BELCASTRO	Sheffield	Points Euro Bantam Title
August 17	v ANTONIO PICARDI	Sheffield	TKO 3rd Euro Bantam Defence
October 12	v FREDDY CRUZ	Sheffield	TKO 6thWBC Int-Super Bantam Title
November 19	v LAUREANO RAMIREZ	Cardiff	TKO 3rd WBC Super Bantam Defence

1995
January 21	v ARMANDO CASTRO	Glasgow	TKO4th WBC Super Bantam Defence
March 4	v SERGIO RAFAEL LIENDO	Livingston	KO 2nd WBC Super Bantam Defence
May 6	v ENRIQUE ANGELES	Shepton Mallet	KO 2nd WBC Super Bantam Defence
July 1	v JUAN POLO PEREZ	Kensington	KO 2nd WBC Super Bantam Defence
September 30	v STEVE ROBINSON	Cardiff	TKO 8thWBO World Featherweight Title

1996
March 16	v SAID LAWAL	Glasgow	KO 1st WBO Featherweight Defence
June 8	v DANIEL ALICEA	Newcastle	KO 2nd WBO Featherweight Defence
August 31	v MANUEL MEDINA	Dublin	TKO 11thWBO Featherweight Defence
November 9	v REMIGIO MOLINA	Manchester	TKO 2ndWBO Featherweight Defence

1997
February 8	v TOM JOHNSON	London	TKO 8thIBF World Featherweight Title
May 3	v BILLY HARDY	Manchester	TKO 1st IBF & WBO F'weight Defence
July 19	v JUAN CARBRERA	London	TKO 2ndIBF & WBO F'weight Defence
October 11	v JOSE BADILLO	Sheffield	TKO 7thWBO Featherweight Defence
December 19	v KEVIN KELLY	New York	KO 4th WBO Featherweight Defence

1998
April 29	v WILFREDO VASQUEZ	Manchester	TKO 7thWBO Featherweight Defence
October 31	v WAYNE McCULLOUGH	Atlantic City	Points WBO Featherweight Defence

1999
April 10	v PAUL INGLE	Manchester	KO 11thWBO Featherweight Defence

ARE YOU A SKY SPORTS SUPERBRAIN?

CRYPTIC QUIZ

Solve the following clues to work out the names of these top stars from the worlds of snooker, football, cricket, tennis and rugby league ...

1. There are usually fireworks when this fella hits the snooker table.
2. Troublesome Chelsea footballer whose name belies his character.
3. You wouldn't expect this former England cricketer to be quick between the wickets.
4. He's proved he's no chicken when the chips are down on the tennis court.
5. You've got to have thick skin to play for this Yorkshire Rugby League side.

ugly mug

We have tweaked the features of three well-known sports figures and invented three new, ugly mugs. Can you identify these stars?

satellite stars

We have mixed up the names of five well-know sporting celebrities. Solve the anagrams to reveal the stars ...

a) **SURGE DESK RIG** (Tennis)   b) **GOAL FRY CART** (Motor Cycling)
c) **JUST MY COG TREE** (Rugby Union)
d) **WHY DOG TRIKE** (Football)   e) **HURLY PANE** (Rugby League)

Missing Names

Using the two words shown in each case as a clue fit the name of a well known player in the middle to form two popular phrases (see example).
Remember, the spellings are not always correct.

1. SOMETHING   <u>ELS</u>   WHERE (golf)

2. NEW   _____   MINSTER (football)

3. EARL   _____   DAY (Sky TV)

4. GIN   _____   WATCHER (cricket)

5. TOP   _____   GUT (rugby union)

Andy's Brainteaser

1. Which respected golfing veteran did Tiger Woods accuse of 'gamesmanship' in the build-up to the US Masters?

2. India pair Suarav Ganguly and Rahul Dravid set a new batting partnership record in the 1999 World Cup. How many runs did they score – 298, 318 or 338?

3. Which young defender made his England debut in the disappointing 1-1 draw in Bulgaria at the end of the last football season?

ANSWERS ON PAGE 83

WORDSEARCH

Hidden within the grid below are the names of 10 major sporting venues from around the world. How many can you find and do you know which sports they host?

W	A	D	B	N	O	U	C	A	M	P	R
T	E	O	C	H	G	I	Q	R	O	V	O
R	Y	M	X	G	N	J	X	S	N	U	L
E	A	A	B	R	O	A	C	C	T	E	A
N	B	H	W	L	P	K	A	Y	E	A	N
T	O	C	S	A	E	L	N	F	C	D	D
B	B	E	L	F	R	Y	A	I	A	T	G
R	G	K	K	A	S	G	R	G	R	I	A
I	H	C	J	N	R	M	I	H	L	G	R
D	H	A	U	G	U	S	T	A	O	E	R
G	T	W	I	C	K	E	N	H	A	M	O
E	B	T	I	R	P	O	L	O	R	D	S

COMING UP NEXT:

SKY SPORTS RUGBY LEAGUE

WE TAKE YOU BETWEEN THE POSTS AND INTO THE WORLD OF SUPER LEAGUE.

SKY SPORTS RUGBY LEAGUE REVIEW

RUGBY LEAGUE TO TAKE CENTRE STAGE IN 2000

Football in 1998, cricket and rugby union in '99, rugby league in 2000 - it's world cup time! The twelfth Rugby League World Cup takes place in Europe in autumn 2000 with 16 nations taking part - six more than the last finals. The heavyweights and favourites will be holders Australia and New Zealand, with British chances made harder than usual after the decision to compete separately as England, Wales, Scotland and Ireland.

That means each of the host nations will see their own country playing group games on home territory before the final, which will be held at either Cardiff's Millennium Stadium, Murrayfield in Edinburgh or Old Trafford, while Wembley is being rebuilt.

The tournament opener is expected to be England v Australia on October 28, a year after Great Britain went down under for the Tri-Nations series against the Kangaroos and Kiwis. The four separate British nations and France had a series at the same time in a bid to prepare their non-Lions for the impact of international rugby.

Great Britain, inaugural winners in 1954, will not have the chance to repeat that triumph but you can be sure England and Wales will be challenging hard in the latter stages in front of their own fans. England and Australia should progress from their group but Wales will be wary of the threat from the Cook Islands.

"We're happy with the draw," said Wales' Keiron Cunningham. "The Cook Islands are a bit of an unknown quantity and we don't know who the qualifiers are yet, so we're going in blind. But we've got a great coach in Clive Griffiths and our aim is to get through the group stages and take it from there."

GROUP ONE:

ENGLAND (hosts)
Will lose some of their best players to the other British teams but still have enough quality with the likes of Kris Radlinski, Keith Senior and Jason Robinson to challenge the big two. Managed by Sheffield's John Kear.

AUSTRALIA (seeds)
The favourites and holders who should reach the final, at least. Despite the retirement of one of their greatest-ever players, Allan Langer, last season, they have more strength-in-depth than any other country. The likes of Brad Fittler, Laurie Daley and Andrew Johns should flourish.

RUSSIA
Stepped up from the Emerging Nations competition to the real thing but have not played an international in the intervening four years! Have 5,000 players to chose from but need to get organised quickly.

FIJI
With over 3,000 junior players coming through, this may be one World Cup too soon for them to make an impression.

It's World

GROUP TWO:

WALES (hosts)
Lost in the semi-final last time out and will be confident of reaching the last four again, with Iestyn Harris and Anthony Sullivan the stars of the show.

NEW ZEALAND (seeds)
Lost narrowly to Australia in the test match at Sydney in April and will be a real threat. They have world-class players in the Paul brothers, Henry and Robbie, Stacey Jones and Richie Barnett.

COOK ISLANDS
A tiny country but with some big men. St Helens star Kevin Iro and brother Tony (South Sydney) have already pledged their allegiance to the country of their ancestors and more will follow. Could pull off a shock.

QUALIFIER
Italy, Lebanon and Morocco play in the Mediterranean Cup with the winners playing the winners of the Pacific Region play-off between Japan, USA and Canada. Italy are overwhelming favourites with Manly's Anthony Colella, Tony Grimaldi of Gateshead and Cronulla Sharks' Shannon Donato probable recruits.

WORLD CUP 2000 GROUPS

Cup time ... again!

GROUP THREE:

FRANCE (hosts)
Once giants of the world game, they have beaten South Africa, Ireland and Scotland recently and were the last country to win a Test Series against Australia - in 1978! Star man is full-back Freddie Banquet of Villeneave Leopards.

PAPUA NEW GUINEA (seeds)
Have been on the international circuit for 20 years but have made little impact of late. Hope to warm-up with games against NZ Maoris and Australia.

SOUTH AFRICA
Fast-tracked into the World Cup thanks to the promoting skills of Louis Luyt. With an eight-team Premiership at home they have a supply of players but will rely on their Super League exports for guidance.

TONGA
Hoping to play the big three in the build-up to the World Cup, so will have a better idea of their strength then. Have a ten-team domestic Premier competition.

GROUP FOUR:

IRELAND (hosts)
Beat Scotland last season and with Shaun Edwards likely to be making his international farewell, with backing from Wigan duo Gary Connolly and Terry O'Connor, could cause an upset.

SAMOA (seeds)
If New Zealand do not want them, the likes of Apollo Perelini, Vila Matautia and Joe Vagana will all be in the Samoan line-up, massively improving their chances of reaching the last eight.

NEW ZEALAND MAORIS
A highly controversial addition, this racial off-shot of the main Kiwi team has been playing around the Pacific in 13 and Sevens competitions. Should be well organised.

SCOTLAND
Lost both of their first internationals last season but with Dale Laughton, Huddersfield pair Danny Russell and Joe Berry, and Logan Campbell of Hull, they have enough quality to reach the quarter-finals on their World Cup debut.

QUARTER-FINALS:
A
Winner Group One v Runner-up Group Four;
B
Winner Group Two v Runner-up Group Three;
C
Winner Group Three v Runner-up Group Two;
D
Winner Group Four v Runner-up Group One.

SEMI-FINALS:
A v C   D v B.

SKY SPORTS
RUGBY LEAGUE REVIEW

RUGBY LEAGUE's heartland may still be along the M62 corridor, in places like Wigan, Leeds, Bradford and Warrington, but fans got the chance to travel to either end of England in Super League IV when Gateshead Thunder joined London Broncos in the big time. We take a look at how the two 'foreign' teams compare and contrast ...

RUGBY LEAGUE hits the road ... NORTH & SOUTH

THUNDER MAKE LIGHTNING START!

It took years of campaigning and months of preparation, but the people who worked so hard to bring professional rugby league to the North East of England were finally rewarded on March 7, 1999 when Gateshead Thunder ran out at a rain-swept International Stadium to play Leeds Rhinos in their inaugural Super League match. Despite the atrocious weather – plus the major attraction across the Tyne where Newcastle United were playing in the FA Cup Quarter-Finals - 6,000 people paid to watch history being made and they were rewarded by a valiant effort by Shaun McRae's Australian captures.

They lost a bruising battle 24-14 but, three months later, the Thunder were well-placed for a play-off place in their first tilt at the Super League. A marvellous effort by all concerned, especially the impressive imports from down under.

When Gateshead were granted a Super League franchise - in preference to the South Wales bids - they were guaranteed not to be relegated in their first season, even if they finished bottom of the league. That act of mercy was not needed after McRae, sacked by St Helens at the end of 1998 and able to recruit some seasoned Aussie pros to Durham, organised a tough new team.

With Kath Hetherington using her knowledge of the British game and Shane Richardson giving up his job at Cronulla Sharks to become the Thunder's chief executive, Gateshead also have some major talent at the top of their organisation.

But, just as importantly, for six years Mick Holgan had been laying the foundations for the Thunder's arrival in his work as RFL Development Officer for the north-east. Dozens of local schools were playing the game and

teenage talents emerging when McRae and Co arrived. He immediately signed up one of them - second-rower Russell Hugill who became the first Geordie to sign for the Thunder.

"It's given the Academy lads a great spur," said Hugill. "They all now think, 'hang on, I can be as good as Russell' and it's filtering through. The more talented kids want to sign for Gateshead now, not go elsewhere."

Gateshead know that it could take years before the Geordie public become rugby league fanatics but if they produce the goods on the field, the crowds will roll up to watch.

Athletics legend Steve Cram is a big supporter of the Thunder's cause and says: "The north-east is a very passionate area for sport and I'm sure Rugby League will take off up here. Thunder have to be competitive and if they are they will build a sizeable hard core support. The north-east public want to watch the best."

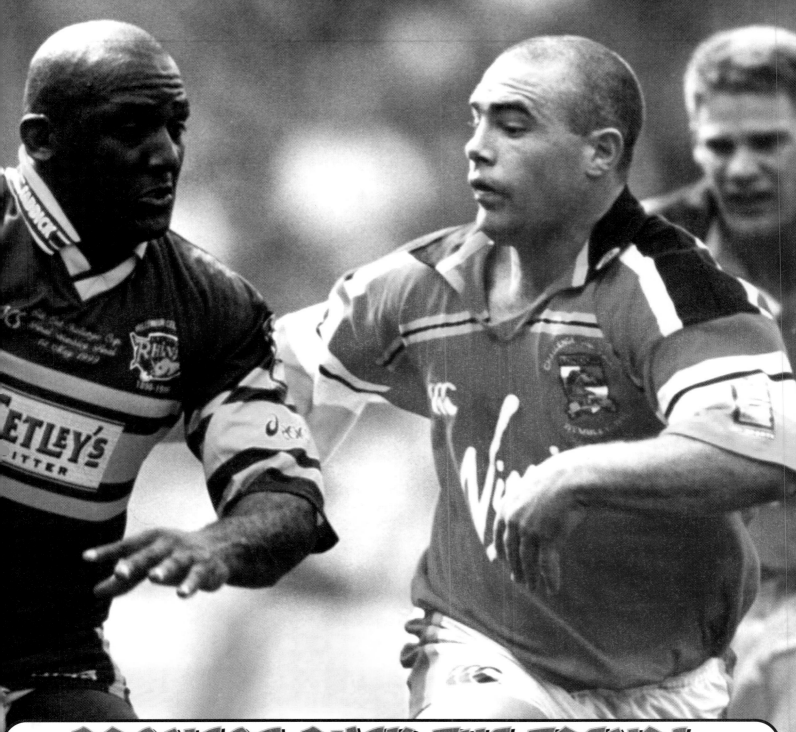

BRONCOS BUCK THE TREND!

After 66 years, four different clubs playing at ten different grounds, several bankruptcies, and efforts way beyond the call of duty, a London rugby league club this year succeeded in reaching the Challenge Cup Final at Wembley. London Broncos may have slumped to the heaviest defeat seen at the Twin Towers after a late onslaught by Leeds Rhinos, but it was a historic and essential occasion for the sport in the south of England.

Twenty years ago, Fulham re-launched Rugby League in the capital, drawing average crowds approaching 10,000 to Craven Cottage. The fact that the Broncos would love to attract the sort of attendance to The Stoop these days indicates how hard it has been to convert Londoners to this great game. But days like the one at Wembley last May made it all worthwhile. London are prospering now under the ownership of Richard Branson's Virgin group, compared to the early 1990s when crowds of

under 300 bothered to watch London Crusaders play at Chiswick. Brisbane Broncos' decision to buy the club, change the name and move them to the Twickenham area via Charlton, may have saved League in London.

Super League chiefs were delighted with London's presence at Wembley, especially when they almost sold out their ticket allocation of 15,000, proving that the expansion policy can work. Those London fans were in heaven when, only minutes after Branson had led his team out, Wembley veteran Martin Offiah pounced on a deflected kick to race away for an exhilarating opening try.

Offiah's place in the Broncos line-up was soon taken by another Londoner, Dominic Peters, the first local to come through the youth ranks into the Super League. But he will not be the last. When Bobby Wallis became the first product of London's rugby league development programme to be selected for Great Britain

Young Lions, he made a major breakthrough for league in the capital. The teenage winger epitomises what Broncos are trying to achieve: build a team who have all graduated to Super League standard through the local schools, Conference and Academy system.

While they do not have to comply to the usual Super League quota of five overseas players, and their star players are mainly Aussies, Wallis has joined an ever-increasing number of Londoners on the Broncos' books. Matt Salter, only 22, Wayne Sykes, Ed Jennings, James Brooks and Steffan Hughes, have all made it into the first team squad after learning the game under inspirational Academy coach Bev Risman.

With Warrington lad Ady Spencer and Tulsen Tollett, born in Sussex but brought up down under, the Broncos could have the basis of an English line-up in a couple of years' time. If that doesn't make fans in Super League's heartland accept and respect London, nothing will.

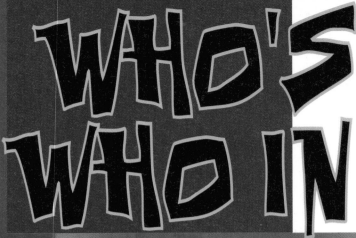

WHO'S WHO IN

SUPER LEAGUE

BRADFORD BULLS

Founded: 1907
Ground: Odsal Stadium (capacity 25,000)
Star players: Henry and Robbie Paul, James Lowes, Leon Pryce, Steve McNamara and Stuart Spruce
Coach: Matthew Elliott (appointed Sept 1996)
Name Game: Changed from Bradford Northern to the Bulls in 1995, influenced by the success of Chicago Bulls basketball team and the cattle fields that skirt the city!

CASTLEFORD TIGERS

Founded: 1926
Ground: Wheldon Road (11,750)
Star players: Danny Orr, Aaron Raper and Dean Sampson
Coach: Stuart Raper (April 1997)
Name Game: Added the Tigers nickname in 1997, a reminder of their yellow and black hooped shirts. Previous nickname - The Glassblowers - is not as appropriate after demise of local industry.

GATESHEAD THUNDER

Founded: 1999
Ground: Gateshead International Stadium (11,800)
Star players: Kerrod Walters, Willie Peters and Matt Daylight
Coach: Shaun McRae (Oct 1998)
Name Game: A new franchise for the North-East in Super League IV, Thunder got their name from a competition in the local community.

HALIFAX BLUE SOX

Founded: 1875 (rugby union club for two years previously)
Ground: New Shay (11,000)
Star players: Graham Holroyd and Paul Broadbent
Coach: John Pendlebury (March 1997)
Name Game: They wear blue socks. What else? They were known as the Thrumhallers but moved from Thrum Hall to ground-share with Halifax Town FC in 1998.

HUDDERSFIELD GIANTS

Founded: 1895 (rugby union club for 30 years previously)
Ground: McAlpine Stadium (25,000)
Star players: Bobby Goulding, Danny Russell and John Bentley
Coach: Malcolm Reilly (Nov 1998)
Name Game: Were known as the Fartowners after their true home ground of Fartown which they left in 1992 for Leeds Road, added the Barracudas nickname in 1984, before settling for Giants in 1998.

HULL SHARKS

Founded: 1895
Ground: Boulevard (11,000)
Star player: Craig Murdock
Coach: Steve Crooks (caretaker May 1999)
Name Game: Previously known as the Airlie Birds, Hull changed to their present marine nickname in 1997 before winning promotion to Super League.

LEEDS RHINOS

Founded: 1870 as St John's, became Leeds 1890
Ground: Headingley (22,000)
Star players: Iestyn Harris, Leroy Rivett, Anthony Farrell, Francis Cummins and Ryan Sheridan
Coach: Dean Lance (Oct 1999)
Name Game: Changed from being 'the Loiners' to 'the Rhinos' in 1997 when Gary Hetherington became Chief Executive. Share their ground with Leeds Tykes rugby union club.

LONDON BRONCOS

Founded: 1980 (as Fulham)
Ground: The Stoop (10,000)
Star players: Shaun Edwards, Karle Hammond, Tulsen Tollett and Steele Retchless
Coach: Les Kiss (June 1999)
Name Game: When Brisbane Broncos bought the London Crusaders they came up with the current combination of the two names.

SALFORD REDS

Founded: 1896
Ground: The Willows (12,000)
Star players: Darren Brown, Gary Broadbent and David Hulme
Coach: John Harvey (June 1999)
Name Game: Previously known as the Red Devils, Salford are the sole top flight survivors in the Manchester area with the demise of Oldham, Swinton, Leigh and Rochdale.

SHEFFIELD EAGLES

Founded: 1984
Ground: Don Valley Stadium (25,000)
Star players: Daryl Powell, Keith Senior, Karl Lovell and Dale Laughton
Coach: John Kear (May 1997)
Name Game: The 'Eagles' landed in the South Yorkshire city but, despite their Challenge Cup triumph of 1998, have failed to bring the crowds into the Don Valley.

ST HELENS

Founded: 1895
Ground: Knowsley Road (19,100)
Star players: Sonny Nickle, Apollo Perelini, Paul Newlove, Anthony Sullivan, Kevin Iro and Sean Long
Coach: Ellery Hanley (Nov 1998)
Name Game: Retained their traditional name in the Super League revolution but 'Saints' are already famous throughout the world.

WAKEFIELD TRINITY WILDCATS

Founded: 1895
Ground: Belle Vue (10,000)/Oakwell (18,806)
Star players: Adrian Brunker, Glen Tomlinson and Frank Watene
Coach: Andy Kelly (June 1997)
Name Game: The 'Dreadnoughts' became the Wildcats when promoted to Super League for 1999.

WARRINGTON WOLVES

Founded: 1879
Ground: Wilderspool (9,350)
Star players: Alan Hunte, Simon Gillies, Toa Kohe-Love and Danny Farrar
Coach: Darryl van de Velde (March 1997)
Name Game: Always known as The Wire, they became the Wolves for Super League but struggled to show their teeth in the early days of summer rugby.

WIGAN WARRIORS

Founded: 1895s
Ground: Robin Park (25,000)
Star players: Andy Farrell, Simon Haughton, Greg Florimo, Kris Radlinski and Jason Robinson
Coach: Andy Goodway (June 1999)
Name Game: Once known as the Riversiders, they became the Warriors after moving from Central Park to the new JJB Stadium for the 2000 season.

COMING UP NEXT:

WE TURN TO THE MORE SEDATE SPORT OF CRICKET WHERE THE SUNDAY LEAGUE SIDES HAVE TAKEN A LEAF OUT OF RUGBY LEAGUE'S BOOK.

SKY SPORTS CRICKET 1999 REVIEW — CRICKET GOES COLOUR CRAZY!

DERBYSHIRE SCORPIONS

Headquarters: County Ground, Derby (capacity 3,500)
Captain: Dominic Cork
Star players: Phil DeFreitas, Karl Krikken, Michael Slater, Adrian Rollins
One-day trophies: 3
Colours: Sky blue with yellow and white
Name game: Top of the batting order's not bad, and they have a sting in their tail.

DURHAM DYNAMOS

Headquarters: Riverside, Chester-le-Street (7,000)
Captain: David Boon
Star players: John Morris, Michael Foster, Melvyn Betts
One-day trophies: 0
Colours: Navy blue and yellow
Name game: They need plenty of energy for all those long journeys south.

ESSEX EAGLES

Headquarters: County Ground, Chelmsford (5,500)
Captain: Nasser Hussain
Star players: Mark Ilott, Stuart Law, Ronnie Irani, Peter Such
One-day trophies: 7
Colours: Yellow with blue and red
Name game: The Salamanca Eagle, captured by The Essex Regiment during the Napoleonic Wars, is incorporated into their colours. No kidding!

GLAMORGAN DRAGONS

Headquarters: Sophia Gardens, Cardiff (6,500)
Captain: Matthew Maynard
Star players: Robert Croft, Adrian Dale, Steve James
One-day trophies: 1
Colours: Blue and gold
Name Game: As Wales' only representative what else could they be called…the Glamorgan daffodils?

GLOUCESTERSHIRE GLADIATORS

Headquarters: County Ground, Bristol (11,500)
Captain: Mark Alleyne
Star players: Jack Russell, Kim Barnett and Michael Smith
One-day trophies: 2
Colours: Sky blue and black
Name Game: Called the Gladiators because the county was occupied by Romans. Another true story, apparently.

HAMPSHIRE HAWKS

Headquarters: County Ground, Southampton (4,600)
Captain: Robin Smith
Star players: Adrian Aymes, Dimitri Mascarenhas and Shaun Udal
One-day trophies: 6
Colours: Sky blue, gold and white
Name Game: There are some birds of prey living in the New Forest and, just as importantly, Hampshire Hawks sounds cool!

KENT SPITFIRES

Headquarters: St Lawrence Ground, Canterbury (10,000)
Captain: Matthew Fleming
Star players: Mark Ealham, Dean Headley, Martin McCague and Alan Wells
One-day trophies: 9
Colours: Maroon and white
Name Game: Second World War spitfire planes were built in the county – and Kent Killers didn't go down too well with the suits at Lords.

LANCASHIRE LIGHTNING

Headquarters: Old Trafford, Manchester (22,000)
Captain: John Crawley
Star players: Warren Hegg, Ian Austin, Andrew Flintoff, Michael Atherton and Neil Fairbrother
One-day trophies: 15
Colours: Red with navy and green trim
Name Game: Lightning because of the traditional Manchester weather - and they ARE sponsored by an electricity company. Honest!

LEICESTERSHIRE SCORPIONS

Headquarters: Grace Road, Leicester (4,500)
Captain: James Whittaker
Star players: Chris Lewis, Darren Maddy, Alan Mullally and Vince Wells
One-day trophies: 5
Colours: Green and red
Name Game: As with the football team, the Fox runs across the club badge and has always been a symbol of Leicester. Dull, but true.

Your Guide To Britain's One-Day Dazzlers !

MIDDLESEX CRUSADERS

Headquarters: Lords, London (30,500)
Captain: Mark Ramprakash
Star players: Angus Fraser, Mike Roseberry and Phil Tufnell
One-day trophies: 7
Colours: Sky and navy blue
Name Game: A tribute to Richard I's attempts to recapture Jerusalem in the 12th century! Allegedly.

NORTHAMPTONSHIRE STEELBACKS

Headquarters: County Ground, Northampton (7,000)
Captain: Matthew Hayden
Star players: Rob Bailey, Graeme Swann, Devon Malcolm and Mal Loye
One-day trophies: 3
Colours: Maroon and gold
Name Game: The Steelbacks, you will be gagging to know, are the county regiment based in the town.

NOTTINGHAMSHIRE OUTLAWS

Headquarters: Trent Bridge, Nottingham (15,000)
Captain: Jason Gallian
Star players: Vasbert Drakes, Paul Johnson, Tim Robinson, and Paul Franks
One-day trophies: 3
Colours: Green and gold
Name Game: Nottingham is famous for its' outlaws in the forest, including a certain Mr R.Hood of Sherwood Forest.

SOMERSET SABRES

Headquarters: County Ground, Taunton (7,500)
Captain: Jamie Cox
Star players: Andy Caddick, Marcus Trescothick and Mark Lathwell
One-day trophies: 5
Colours: Maroon and white
Name Game: The county was scene of some blood-letting in the Civil War with the Duke of Monmouth's rebel forces being slaughtered by King James' army. Sabres were the favoured weapon of the time. Impressed, eh?

SURREY LIONS

Headquarters: The Oval, London (17,500)
Captain: Adam Hollioake
Star players: Alec Stewart, Ben Hollioake, Graham Thorpe and Alex Tudor
One-day trophies: 4
Colours: Dark blue, red and yellow
Name Game: They hope to roar their way back to the top of the English game. Plus, most of their players play for England anyway.

SUSSEX SHARKS

Headquarters: County Ground, Hove (6,800)
Captain: Chris Adams
Star players: Robin Martin-Jenkins, Tony Cottey and Justin Bates
One-day trophies: 5
Colours: Blue and gold
Name Game: Based on the seaside, what else could Sussex call themselves? Apart from the Sussex Shrimpers, that is.

WARWICKSHIRE BEARS

Headquarters: Edgbaston, Birmingham (18,000)
Captain: Neil Smith
Star players: Nick Knight, Allan Donald, Dougie Brown and Ed Giddins
One-day trophies: 9
Colours: Navy blue and gold
Name Game: Bears have always been the county's symbol of defiance. Don't ask us why, they just have. Okay?

WORCESTERHIRE ROYALS

Headquarters: New Road, Worcester (5,200)
Captain: Tom Moody
Star players: Graeme Hick, Steve Rhodes and Phil Newport
One-day trophies: 5
Colours: Green and black
Name Game: The city is famous for its Royal Worcester crockery, Charles II led his troops at the Battle of Worcester in 1651 and Prince Arthur's Chantry is the city's richest monument. Enough reasons?

YORKSHIRE PHOENIX

Headquarters: Headingley, Leeds (18,000)
Captain: David Byas
Star players: Darren Gough, Matthew Wood, Gavin Hamilton and Craig White
One-day trophies: 4
Colours: Dark blue, light blue and gold
Name Game: They hope to rise from ashes and win their first one-day league since 1983. Or did they get shot down in flames?

GOUGHIE
a footballer's cricketer ...

"BIG LAD, BIG SMILE, BIG PACE ..."
David Lloyd

DAVID Gower was perhaps the ultimate cricketer's cricketer. Good at his job and a real gentleman to boot. Ian Botham, meanwhile, was much more in yer face. Great at his job but a bit of a lad.

The way Darren Gough plays the game suggests he may be a one-off hybrid of the two, perhaps with a bit of Paul Gascoigne thrown in. A self-styled footballing cricketer of the people. That's his quote, not ours!

And quite a cricketer he is too. At the end of March, he picked up his second Cornhill Test Cricketer of the Year award after an Ashes series which has catapulted the 28-year-old Yorkshireman firmly into the category of world-class paceman, alongside Allan Donald, Glenn McGrath and the veteran Courtney Walsh.

He didn't have a bad World Cup either. Shame the England batsmen could not match the bowling performances of both Goughie and strike partner Alan Mullaly. His batting may have failed to live up to its early all-rounder billing, but his growing army of fans will forgive him for that.

His pace with ball in hand and passion for the game in general have made him a real favourite; not just amongst supporters but selectors who live in fear of another injury to their main assault weapon. Not bad for a lad who was picked for the A team tour to South Africa five years as a 'possible third seamer'.

Former England coach David Lloyd, whose outspoken ways suggested he didn't mind a touch of feisty footballer in cricketer's whites, liked to describe Goughie as: "Big lad, big smile, big pace." Big heart too...

GOUGHIE ON HIS BACKGROUND

I was more of a footballer at heart when I was a kid. I grew up in a tough part of Barnsley where you had to fight or be bullied. If you couldn't look after yourself you were nothing. Because I was the football, cricket, athletics and rugby captain, they picked on me more than the rest. I reckon it was good for me. It gave me a good attitude. Mind you, they still take the mickey out of me because I can't always talk my way out of arguments like the others. I'm what you might call a footballer's cricketer. I grew up playing football with football people and to be honest, I preferred it to cricket. I was on the YTS at Rotherham and some of my friends have made it as pro footballers. And if somebody had guaranteed me a Premier club, I would have gone for football. But I've got no regrets about choosing cricket. I made the right choice."

GOUGHIE ON CHILDREN

"I've got two sons and they've changed everything in my life. They're great. My little one is huge for his age and will be big, physically awesome. My older one has got a tremendous eye already so perhaps he could be a decent bat. He copies everything I do, watches all my videos. But it isn't always easy because they take up so much time and energy. I don't know if we'll have any more...sometimes it's a relief to go on tour for a break!

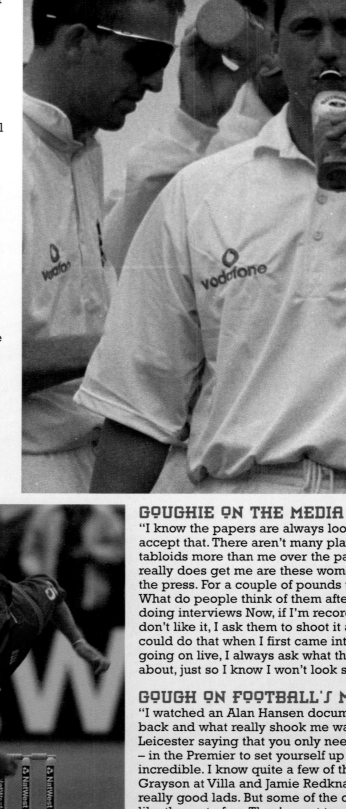

GOUGHIE ON THE MEDIA

"I know the papers are always looking for stories and I can accept that. There aren't many players who've been in the tabloids more than me over the past couple of years. But what really does get me are these women who sell their stories to the press. For a couple of pounds they ruin their reputations. What do people think of them afterwards? But I don't mind doing interviews Now, if I'm recording an interview and I don't like it, I ask them to shoot it again. I didn't realise you could do that when I first came into the game. And if I'm going on live, I always ask what they're going to question me about, just so I know I won't look stupid."

GOUGH ON FOOTBALL'S MILLIONAIRES

"I watched an Alan Hansen documentary on the telly a while back and what really shook me was Robbie Savage of Leicester saying that you only need one contract – four years – in the Premier to set yourself up for life. I think it's incredible. I know quite a few of the footballers – Simon Grayson at Villa and Jamie Redknapp at Liverpool and they're really good lads. But some of the others, well, they're just not like the rest of us. They've got too much, I reckon."

GOUGHIE ON THE WORLD CUP

I don't think people realised just what a huge event it was going to be once the football season was over. It's just a shame we let ourselves down and didn't keep the home interest going longer than we did. We started off okay but didn't do it when it really mattered, and that's disappointing. We really wanted to do well to help raise the profile of the game – and give our fans something to shout about.

SKY SPORTS CRICKET

Aussies On Top Of The World Thanks To Super Shane!

1999 REVIEW

PAKISTAN WARNE OUT!

Written off by many as an over-weight has-been, Australian spin doctor Shane Warne had the last laugh by setting up a thoroughly deserved World Cup victory for his country with a bowling performance which rammed the cruel taunts of his detractors firmly down their throats once and for all.

Little more than six months before his greatest triumph, and there have been a few, Warne was being told by experts and the cricketing public alike that he would never be the same player again after undergoing an operation for a serious shoulder injury. But, like many great sporting stars before him, the durable Aussie proved beyond doubt that he is still the king of spin by bouncing back with two match-winning performances when they mattered most; in the semi-final nail-biter with South Africa and the Cup Final cruise against poor Pakistan.

Wasim Akram and his men had looked awesome in their run-up to the final, but the Pakis peaked too soon and looked simply Warne-out by the time they reached Lords. By the end of a one-sided contest which took less than 60 overs to decide, they were positively on their knees.

So instead of scorn, it was unanimous praise which was being poured over the Australian maestro whose devastating 4-33 ripped out Pakistan's middle order to win the Man of the Match award for himself and the title of World Champions for his country at the end of a tournament which ebbed and flowed without ever being a storming success. Warne, who said he was considering quitting international cricket after his final flourish, said: "Not long back I was written off after undergoing a major shoulder operation, but I have gradually got better and better and in the final managed to break the back of the Pakistani side.

"But I'm not going to say anything about the people who wrote me off. I never go out to prove anyone wrong. I go out there and play because I love the big stage and I love playing for my country."

And he did it brilliantly to finish as the tournament's joint-leading wicket taker on 20 with New Zealand's Geoff Allott. Not that humbled Pakistan skipper Akram was surprised. "A lot of people had written off Warne, but I was not one of them," he said. "He is still the best spinner in the world." Anyone want to argue with that now?

WORLD CUP HEADLINERS

BEST BOWLING FIGURES
1 Glenn McGrath (Australia)   5-14 v West Indies
2 Lance Klusener (South Africa)   5-21 v Kenya
3 Venkatesh Prasad (India)   5-27 v Pakistan
4 Rabindra Singh (India)   5-31 v Sri Lanka
5 Saqlain Mushtaq (Pakistan)   5-35 v Bangladesh

HIGHEST SCORERS
1 Saurav Ganguly (India)   183 v Sri Lanka
2 Rahul Dravid (India)   145 v Sri Lanka
3 Sachin Tendulkar (India)   140 not out v Kenya
4 Neil Johnson (Zimbabwe)   132 not out v Australia
5 Steve Waugh (Australia)   120 not out v South Africa

TOP RUN MAKERS
1 Rahul Dravid (India)		461
2 Steve Waugh (Australia)		398
3 Saurav Ganguly (India)		379
4 Mark Waugh (Australia)		375
5 Neil Johnson (Zimbabwe)		367

TOP WICKET TAKERS
1 Geoff Allott (New Zealand)		20
1 Shane Warne (Australia)		20
3 Glenn McGrath (Australia)		18
4 Lance Klusener (South Africa)		17
4 Saqlain Mushtaq (Pakistan)		17

DO AN ANDY GRAY...

COMPETITION TIME

...GIVE IT A TOUCH OF TYLER...

WIN!

HOW TO WIN!

To stand a chance of winning this unique competition, all you have to do is name your favourite sporting event of the year; one which you would like to watch from the luxury of the Sky Studios – and then commentate on later. So get thinking and the first TEN entries pulled out of the hat will get to spend a day at the Sky Sports studios in West London. You will be able to take away a video recording of your efforts, together with a few suitable Sky goodies. So start filling in the form opposite now…

Send your entries to:
Sky "Favourite Sport"
Competition,
Pedigree Books Ltd,
The Old Rectory,
Matford Lane,
Exeter EX2 4PS

Closing date: February 28, 2000

★ A DAY AT THE SKY SPORTS STUDIOS
★ WATCH A LIVE EVENT ON SKY'S BIG SCREEN
★ DO A MINI VOICE-OVER ON THE OCCASION
★ TAKE AWAY A VIDEO RECORDING OF YOUR COMMENTARY
★ LOTS OF OTHER SKY GOODIES

YOUR NAME ....
ADDRESS ....
....
....
AGE ....
PHONE NUMBER ....
MY FAVOURITE SPORTING EVENT :
....
....
....

BASKETBALL REVIEW

BUDDY

SHEFFIELD TAKE BUDWEISER TITLE IN THRILLING FINALE

IT was the most exciting season in the history of British basketball. In the last year of its old format, before switching to an American-style regional Conference system for 1999-2000, the professional game saw record crowds, a new team take a firm foothold north of the border, increased TV viewing figures and, most importantly of all, some breathtakingly exciting basketball.

The National Cup was decided on Terrell Myers' buzzer-beating shot that gave the Sheffield Sharks the slenderest of victories against underdogs the London Leopards, while the Derby Storm reached their first ever final and led mighty Manchester Giants at half-time of the uniball Trophy decider only to slip off after the break as the absence of suspended Yorick Williams and Rico Alderson took effect.

The Wembley Championships were all about upsets as first and second seeds Sheffield and Manchester were KO'd in the semi-finals by London Towers and Thames Valley Tigers who fought out an all-south Final with honours going to the Towers.

And, most memorable of all, Manchester and Sheffield met at the MEN Arena on Good Friday, the final day of the regular season, with their records tied at the top of the Budweiser League. The equation was simple, whoever won the game won the League and more than 11,000 fans poured into the arena to witness a little piece of history being made. The game, and the occasion, did not disappoint. The contest see-sawed one way, then the other, until the Sharks seemed to have established a commanding lead late in the game. Manchester rallied one last time to tie the scores and set up a breathtaking finale. With one last possession, Myers had the ball stripped under the Manchester basket, resulting in a Sheffield possession with HALF a second left in the game, and the season. From the in-bounds pass, a fatal lapse in concentration by the Manchester defence saw the ball reach Myers who hit the winning basket with his usual deadly precision. "It was probably the best game ever staged in this country," said Manchester coach Nick Nurse after the disappointment subsided. "I think it was a powerful statement about how far the game has come in this country as a viable professional sport. Of course, it would have been a better statement for me if the Giants had won, but, looking back now, that doesn't matter as much as the importance of the actual event."

The Sharks with the Budweiser Championship trophy after their incredible last-second triumph over the Giants.

BRILLIANT!

Nurse's Giants started the season as hot favourites to sweep all before them after a summer of big spending landed them established domestic stars like Tony Dorsey, Tony Holley and John White. But it quickly emerged that northern rivals the Sharks were going to have a great deal to say in the distribution of prizes. Chris Finch's well-oiled team set off on a 13-match unbeaten start to the season that was only ended, in early November, by an upstart Derby Storm who were quickly emerging themselves as a genuine trophy contender. Their young, brash American coach Bob Donewald, recognised as one of the most brilliant and fiery bosses in the business, had assembled a team of unknown Americans and journeymen British players, with the added ingredient of former Giant Yorick Williams.

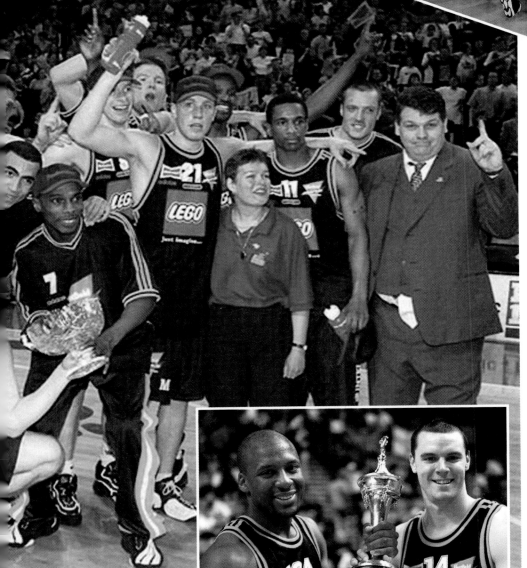

The Manchester Giants celebrate their uniball Trophy triumph (above).

Sheffield Sharks' stars Wil Johnson and Todd Cauthorn with the National Cup.

Derby, who always played an aggressive, passionate style of basketball, saw their season unravel at Chester after the turn of the year when Williams and team mate Rico Alderson were involved in a brawl with Chester's Shaun Hartley that caused the game to be abandoned. The three players were handed season-long bans as the authorities handed out the stiffest punishments in the history of the game. By the time the suspensions came into effect, the Storm had booked their place in the uniball Trophy Final where the loss of their two key starters ultimately allowed Manchester a comfortable 90-69 win, the Giants' first honour in 12 years and a result that eased the pressure on Nurse who had been expected to deliver in his first season. A sign of Derby's huge improvement was the fact they beat the Sharks in two of their three league encounters, but they were one of the few teams able to challenge Finch's side. Even though the Yorkshiremen lost gifted American Matt Gaudio to a career-ending knee ligament injury before Christmas, they picked up England veteran Peter Scantlebury from Newcastle and barely missed a beat. Scants' was cup-tied for the National Cup campaign but watched from the sidelines as the Sharks cruised past Thames Valley in the semis and won the thrilling Final with the Leopards 67-65. "It truly was a great season," said Finch. "We want this club to be consistently competing for honours season after season and I think we can say we have reached that level. We want to be the Manchester United of basketball."

SKY SPORTS

BASKETBALL REVIEW

ALL CHANGE PLEASE!

The coming season will see the big two – the Sharks and the Giants - and the other 11 teams fight out a new format with the league split into North and South Conferences. The top four teams from each Conference will enter the play-offs, with four clubs advancing to the Finals at Wembley. The aim is to clarify the uncertainty over whether the League winners or Play-off winners deserve the title 'Champions'. "I like this system," said Nurse, who has already installed his Giants as favourites to win the first Championship of the new millennium. "It follows the American example and puts even greater emphasis on Wembley as an event. It is going to make for another exciting season."

PLAYER OF THE SEASON
TERRELL MYERS
(SHEFFIELD SHARKS)

Twice the American guard found the ball in his hands with time running out in trophy-winning situations; twice Myers shot the ball; twice it went in, so winning the Budweiser League and National Cup for his Sharks. Myers (in action right) emerged as the coolest head and coolest pair of hands in the British game, drawing comparisons with the great Michael Jordan. "I told the guys, get me the ball and I'll score," said Myers after he beat Manchester in the title decider. They did, and he did!

COACH OF THE SEASON
CHRIS FINCH
(SHEFFIELD SHARKS)

Two years into his reign as Sheffield leader, Finch now has three trophies to his name and is rapidly emerging as the heir to Kevin Cadle's crown as the king of coaches. A shrewd recruiter and judge of talent, Finch also matured in his man-management style, making the Sharks the closest-knit group in the game. They lacked the talent of the Giants, but had the spirit and heart.

BAD BOY OF THE SEASON
BOB DONEWALD
(DERBY STORM coach)

Love him or hate him, one thing you could not do to Derby's extrovert coach Bob Donewald was ignore him. From his questionable taste in clothes to his brilliant, brash style of basketball, Donewald was a breath of fresh air to the British game - although the authorities tended to disagree, as did Derby who did not renew his contract despite leading the team to the best year in their history.

TEAM OF THE SEASON
SHEFFIELD SHARKS

The season ended on a low note with Sheffield performing their usual disappearing act in the Wembley Championships, but this was the year of the Shark in British basketball. A League and Cup double in Chris Finch's second year as coach, despite the mid-season loss to career-ending injury of influential American Matt Gaudio, spelled nothing but success.

WHO WON WHAT?

Budweiser League:
SHEFFIELD SHARKS
Budweiser Championships
(play-offs): **LONDON TOWERS**
National Cup:
SHEFFIELD SHARKS
uniball Trophy:
MANCHESTER GIANTS
Budweiser MVP Award:
DANNY LEWIS
(London Towers)

MVP Danny Lewis

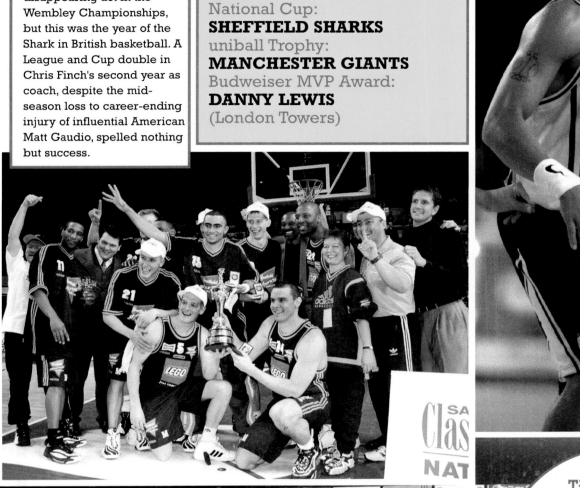

GAME OF THE SEASON
MANCHESTER V SHEFFIELD

The top teams in the League met on the final day of the season with the winners taking the title. With half a second remaining in the season, Terrell Myers hit the winning basket (left) to clinch an 87-85 victory that meant heartache for the Giants' fans in the 11,000-plus crowd at the MEN Arena. Not just game of the season, probably the greatest game of all-time in British basketball.

SKY SPORTS
CROSSWORD 2

CLUES ACROSS:

7   You shouldn't overstep this mark in darts (4)
8   Dynamos from the cricketing North East (6)
10 Olympic venue in 1996 (7)
11 Rhinos who triumphed over Broncos at Wembley in '99 (5)
12 Italian coach and most-capped footballer – christian name (4)
13 You need to have this in whatever sport you play (5)
17 Top American golfer this year (5)
18 Friendly score in tennis (4)
22 Delivery in baseball (5)
23 Soccer's European Championship hosts in 1996 (7)
24 Anil, one of India's many talented spinners (6)
25 Take a penalty from here (4)

CLUES DOWN:

1   Captain of Rugby League's Challenge Cup runners-up this year (7)
2   Irish boxer whose comeback to the ring was hampered by injury (7)
3   Tricky Aussie bowler – you have been warned (5)
4   One of few English successes at this year's cricket World Cup (7)
5   Number of trophies Alex Ferguson got to grips with last season (3)
6   Punishing shot in tennis (5)
9   Ryder Cup leader (4,5)
14 Another cup teams battle for in golf (7)
15 Not just a fair weather racer on two wheels (7)
16 Football club which left Elm Park for a spanking new stadium (7)
19 Part of a sprinter's footwear (5)
20 Victorious cricketers like one as a souvenir (5)
21 England beat these African soccer minnows in the 1990 World Cup finals (5)

SKY SPORTS

1998 1999

FOOTBALL REVIEW

TOO MANY OF TODAY'S REFS WANT TO MAKE NAMES FOR THEMSELVES. THE GAME IS ABOUT PLAYERS, NOT FAME-SEEKING OFFICIALS !

A is for ... **ALCOCK, PAUL** who stumbled (literally) across fame in one of the most bizarre incidents of the season at Hillsborough last September. Struggling to control a tempestuous encounter between Sheffield Wednesday and Arsenal, the Durham official had the temerity to upset Italian hot-head Paolo Di Canio who saw red in more ways than one. After being dismissed by referee Alcock, Di Canio decided to take the law into his own hands (literally) by pushing the man in black to the ground by way of demonstrating his disgust. Clearly, not the most sensible thing to do but the nature of Mr Alcock's fall would not have looked out of place on the set of an old Hollywood movie where the wounded victim staggers around the stage before falling in a customary heap. All very amusing for the on-lookers although not quite as funny as the heavily suspended and fined Di Canio's remarks some time later when he accused Mr Alcock of taking a dive! Now there's a turn up for the book.

A is also for ...
AMORUSO, LORENZO
who was a target for the Ibrox boo boys at the start of the season but was being hailed a hero by the end of it as he led Glasgow Rangers to a glorious treble in coach Dick Advocaat's first year in charge. You can say what you like about the standard of Scottish football, but three trophies in one season in any league is still some achievement. Not quite as good as Manchester United, but ...

LORENZO AMORUSO

B is for ... **BERGKAMP, DENNIS** who enjoyed another exceptional season in the race for the Premiership title, helping Arsenal push rivals Manchester United all the way to the line. Sublime skills and, once again, some wonderful goals further underlined his importance to the Gunners, but it was Bergkamp's reluctance to fly to away games which ultimately cost Arsene Wenger the chance of a serious stab at the Champions League. Without him Arsenal are not the same potent force and it showed in their results overseas and the Highbury faithful can only hope the great man can overcome this particular phobia. They need him.

B is also for ... **BASSETT, DAVE** who was given the heave-ho by Nottingham Forest when really it should have been Dutch dissenter Pierre Van Hooijdonk who should have been kicked out of the City Ground for his selfish, one-man strike at the start of last season. His actions were a major factor behind the club's ultimate demise and did nothing to help Bassett keep the club in the Premier; and himself in a job. Next stop Barnsley.

TO THE MEN THEIR MARK

C is for ... **COLLYMORE, Stanley**
who became the latest high profile player to seek counselling for stress and depression after losing his way on the field and losing the plot off it. Despite getting a so-called 'dream move' to Aston Villa and having an understanding boss in the shape of John Gregory, Collymore still couldn't find the sort of form which once led people to believe he could be a world beater; England's very own Ronaldo. At a time when players like Paul Merson and Paul Gascoigne were struggling to come to terms with their own particular problems, the Collymore situation once again raised the issue of players and pressure. But, even amongst the Villa fans, there was little in the way of sympathy for sad Stan.

C is also for ... **COLE, Andy**
who went a hell of a long way towards proving a hell of a lot of people wrong about his finishing ability. His free-scoring partnership with Dwight Yorke had Coley smiling too and their goals, around 50 in all, played a major part in Manchester United's treble triumph. Shame for the former Newcastle striker that the season ended on a bum note with another disappointing England performance against Sweden to raise all the old doubts.

D is for ... **DAVIES, David**
whose head was held high while others were rolling at Lancaster Gate, giving him a very powerful voice within the Football Association who ended the tenures of chief executive Graham Kelly and head coach Glenn Hoddle, amongst others. It was suggested that Hoddle, who upset all and sundry with his ill-judged comments about disabled people, had parted company with the FA by mutual consent but after a series of gaffs the powers-that-be clearly believed enough was enough. No question about his ability as a coach; no question about his commitment, but Hoddle didn't do himself any favours at times with personal comments about things none-football. His relationship with the media too could have been better; and may have saved him. Howard Wilkinson stepped into the breach for a while, but King Kev was the man they all wanted. But for how long?

D is also for ... **DALGLISH, Kenny**
who became the first managerial casualty of the last Premiership season when he was sacked by Newcastle before the summer tans had faded. The club said Dalglish had offered to resign; Dalglish said the club had fired him to appoint Ruud Gullit and an unholy row ensued. But by the end of the season Dalglish was smiling again, back in the bosom of his first club Celtic as the main man, with John Barnes at his side.

ANDY COLE

SKY SPORTS
1998 1999
FOOTBALL REVIEW

F is for ... **FERGUSON, Alex**

who can now justifiably claim the title of Manchester United's most successful manager from the legendary Sir Matt Busby after guiding the club to an historic treble, made up of the FA Carling Premiership, the FA Cup and the European Cup – the most important of all. Fergie was suitably rewarded by United with a new, mega-bucks contract which will take him up to his announced retirement date when he's 60, and best of all he was awarded an OBE for his incredible achievements as a manager, not just with United but his former club Aberdeen who he also guided to European glory. And who's to say that, with the current crop of relatively young players at Old Trafford signed up on long-term contracts, United will not continue to rule at home and abroad for years to come.

F is also for ... **FILAN, John**

who successfully ousted former England keeper Tim Flowers from the number one spot at Ewood Park, but could not keep Blackburn Rovers in the Premiership after a season which lurched from one disaster to another. Not even the arrival of Alex Ferguson's number two Brian Kidd could provide the spur for the club which fell as quickly as it rose.

E is for ... **EVANS, Roy**

who ultimately paid the price for being 'too nice' and became the last of the original boot room brigade at Anfield to part company with Liverpool. Evans, a bit like Dave Bassett who took the rap for his players' failings, had been at Anfield since he was a teenager, playing, coaching and managing before walking away to leave the task to his short-term managerial partner Gerard Houllier. The idea of the educated Frenchman and the loveable scouser working in unison sounded good in principle but was destined to fail and it was no great surprise when Evans was asked to hand over the reins to Houllier who made massive changes in the summer in a determined bid to arrest Liverpool's dramatic decline.

E is also for ... **ELTON John**

who watched via satellite from Seattle as his beloved Watford were led back to the top flight by his beloved Graham Taylor. The musical millionaire was positively ecstatic as he heaped praise on the First Division underdogs who beat Bolton in an exciting play-off final at Wembley. He was also glowing in his praise for Taylor who once again proved what a good club manager he is. As for England....

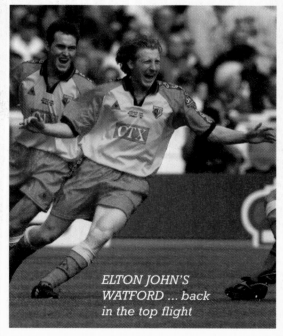

ELTON JOHN'S WATFORD ... back in the top flight

IT TOOK ALEX TEN YEARS TO GET HIS TEAM – AND HIS SQUAD – EXACTLY THE WAY HE WANTS IT, BUT LAST SEASON'S ACHIEVEMENT WAS SIMPLY MONUMENTAL !

ALEX FERGUSON

G is for ... GIGGS, Ryan and GINOLA, David

who scored two of the goals of a memorable season, both in sensational solo fashion. Manchester United ace Giggs' wonder goal in the FA Cup semi-final replay against Arsenal was described by many as the greatest ever in the history of the competition (although Ricky Villa might have something to say about that). But while the Welsh wizard's match-winning strike was about pace and purpose, Ginola's magical goal against Barnsley was the wonderful result of brilliance and balance. Some opponents have criticised Ginola for diving, but there is no denying his supreme ability and he was duly rewarded for a season of consistency by being named both the PFA and the Football Writers' Player of the Season (although Dwight Yorke might have something to say about that).

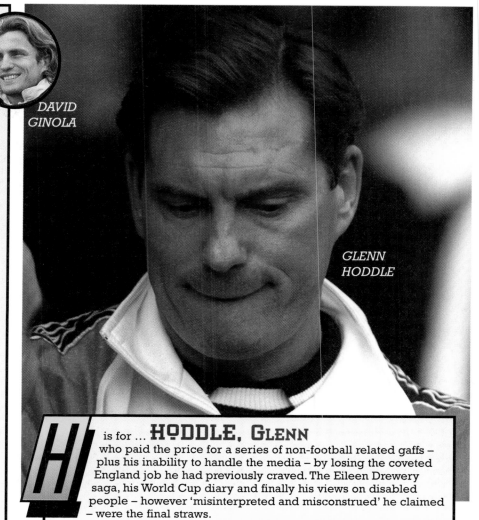

DAVID GINOLA

RYAN GIGGS

GLENN HODDLE

G is also for ... GLASS, Jimmy

who helped soccer scribes write arguably THE story of the season by scoring the goal, with virtually the last kick of the campaign, which kept lowly Carlisle in the Nationwide League and sent Scarborough back to the Conference. Even more amazing, Glass is a goalkeeper who was playing his last game on loan with the

H is for ... HODDLE, Glenn

who paid the price for a series of non-football related gaffs – plus his inability to handle the media – by losing the coveted England job he had previously craved. The Eileen Drewery saga, his World Cup diary and finally his views on disabled people – however 'misinterpreted and misconstrued' he claimed – were the final straws.

LEE HUGHES

> LEE IS A GREAT TALENT AND CLEARLY A NATURAL GOALSCORER WHO WILL GO ON TO BETTER THINGS. AS FOR MARK, I KNOW HIS GOAL-SCORING RETURN FOR THE SAINTS WAS PRETTY NAFF, BUT HIS OVERALL CONTRIBUTION IN KEEPING THE CLUB UP WAS IMMENSE !

H is for ... HUGHES, Lee

who was the only player in England to score over 30 League goals last season – and all this in a West Brom side capable of achieving little more than a mid-table position in the First Division. Not surprisingly, Hughes attracted the attention of the Premiership big boys with his goalscoring exploits and he also won himself a spanking new sports car for his efforts; hitting a 25-goal target before Christmas. While young Lee was hammering in the goals left, right and centre, namesake Mark went through a full 48 hours of football action before getting on the scoresheet for Southampton following the veteran striker's move from Chelsea in the summer of '98.

I is for ... IMPEY, ANDY

whose transfer from West Ham to Leicester in the early part of the season infuriated Hammers' generally easy-going boss Harry Redknapp because the deal had gone on behind his back. Having earlier denied that Impey was on his way to Filbert Street, Redknapp was forced to concede a deal had gone through without his knowledge or consent. Harry's wobbler wasn't quite on a par with Kevin Keegan's televised ranting on Sky when Alex Ferguson's gamesmanship got the better of him, but it was close. It wasn't the only transfer to take place behind a manager's back and Everton boss Walter Smith was also to discover that a chairman's word is not always his bond when Duncan Ferguson was sold to Newcastle for £7m in similar, if not more controversial, circumstances.

I is also for ... ILIC, SASA

who had booked Charlton's place in the Premiership at the end of the previous season with a couple of penalty shoot-out saves in the dramatic play-off final with Sunderland, but failed to live up to his early promise once in the top flight. Serb Ilic may have been preoccupied with problems in his homeland as Charlton fought in vain to preserve their Premiership status.

J is for ... JEFFERS, FRANCIS

who was one of few Merseyside successes throughout a troubled campaign for fallen giants Everton and Liverpool. Not exactly your soccer star pin-up and with more fat on him than you see on the average chip, but this boy has talent and he proved it on a number of occasions – even in a struggling side. He has the uncanny ability to beat players at will, pretty much in the way Steve McManaman used to do for Everton's great rivals across Stanley Park, and the England Under-21 international also proved he has a keen eye for goal. His performances, together with the dramatic impact made by goal hero Kevin Campbell at the death, helped keep the Goodison men up and provide at least some hope for a brighter future.

PAUL JEWELL

Nationwide FOOTBALL LEAGUE WE'RE GOING UP!

FRANCIS JEFFERS

IT'S OFTEN SAID THAT THE INFLUX OF FOREIGN PLAYERS WILL HAMPER THE PROGRESS OF YOUNG, HOMEGROWN TALENT, BUT JEFFERS IS ONE OF A NUMBER OF EXCEPTIONS TO THAT RULE !

J is for ... JEWELL, PAUL

who brilliantly guided outside bets Bradford to automatic promotion from Division One in his first full season as a manager. Jewell, who became the Premiership's youngest ever boss, knows he is still learning the management game but Bradford have clearly unearthed a gem.

KEVIN KEEGAN

HENRIK LARSSON

K is for … **KEEGAN, KEVIN**
whose infectious enthusiasm, passion for the game and man-management skills made him the nation's favourite to replace Glenn Hoddle as England coach. Having brilliantly lifted Fulham out of the doldrums, Keegan allowed his patriotic heart to rule his head by accepting the England job full-time after originally promising to see out his contract and see through his dream at Craven Cottage. A convincing and entertaining 3-0 win at home to Poland in his first international as the official leader was followed by two Euro 2000 disappointments by way of lack-lustre performances at home to Sweden and away to Bulgaria, both games ending in draws. But Keegan promised that he will get it right….eventually.

K is also for … **KEWELL, HARRY**
who was one of a number of young players to benefit from the more attacking, ambitious policies of Leeds United boss David O'Leary who removed the defensive shackles from his eager youngsters following the departure of George Graham to Spurs. And with devastating effect too, guiding the club into Europe at the first attempt with Aussie Kewell and striker Alan Smith, in particular, outstanding.

L is for … **LAUDRUP, BRIAN**
who was the envy of football followers, indeed the majority of the game's well-paid stars, when he successfully negotiated a staggering £50,000 a week deal with Chelsea after exercising the option of a Bosman free move from Rangers. But Laudrup's time at Stamford Bridge, after enjoying so much success with the Glasgow giants, was a miserable one and he never came to terms with Gianluca Vialli's so-called rotation system. A few months of moaning and whingeing later, homesick Laudrup decided he wanted to go back home to Denmark where he took a massive pay cut to play for the country's leading club FC Copenhagen. Still not content with life, Laudrup walked out on the club at the end of the season and is currently seeking happiness in Amsterdam with Ajax.

> WHEN YOU BUY QUALITY FOREIGN PLAYERS YOU ARE OFTEN BUYING SOME EXCESS BAGGAGE TOO. BUT BRIAN LAUDRUP'S ACTIONS SURPRISED ME BECAUSE I HAD HIM DOWN AS ONE OF THE MORE RELIABLE ONES !

L is also for … **LARSSON, HENRIK**
who was the leading scorer in the Scottish Premiership by a mile but still couldn't help Celtic close the gap on treble-winners Rangers. But the arrival of Kenny Dalglish and John Barnes at Celtic Park in the summer has instilled fresh hope at the club where 'King Kenny' was a hero as a player.

SKY SPORTS
1998 1999
FOOTBALL REVIEW

is for ... **NIELSEN, Allan**
who won the Worthington Cup for Spurs with a dramatic, last-minute Wembley winner which broke the hearts of opponents Leicester, especially veteran striker Tony Cottee who is still looking for his first winners' medal after a long and distinguished career littered with goals but not trophies. No such lack of success for Tottenham's new manager George Graham, however, and he began his stint with Spurs in exactly the same way as he began his spell in charge of Arsenal; by lifting the League Cup. Nielsen, like many of his Tottenham colleagues, played like a man-possessed; a far cry from the ram-shackled days of indiscipline before the arrival of Graham. If the tough, taskmaster carries on in such a positive vain then the fact he once managed 'the other lot' across North London with such distinction may yet be forgotten. But then again...

is also for ... **NEVILLE, Gary and Philip**
who more than played their part in Manchester United's glorious, all-conquering campaign. Perhaps not as brash as Beckham or as grand as Giggs, but the way they go about their tasks with such quiet, efficiency is well recognised by Alex Ferguson and the Old Trafford faithful. They're brothers, you know!

M is for ...
McMANAMAN, Steve
whose transfer to Real Madrid may well NOT have gone through had his agents not secured a pre-contractual agreement with the Spanish bosses who, despite snapping up the Liverpool striker on a Bosman free, might have thought twice about paying Macca a king's ransom after arguably his worst season at Anfield. The England international's mind might well have been on his lucrative contract (reported to be in excess of £60,000-a-week with customary added extras) with Real long before the end of the Premiership season judging by some of his lack-lustre performances. You can hardly blame McManaman for cashing in on the new player-power ruling, or for wanting to take up the challenge of playing in the Primera Liga, but Liverpool fans were clearly not happy with the player's closing contributions. But it all ended amicably with Macca signing off with a goal and leaving the field to a standing ovation in his final game for the Merseyside club.

STEVE McMANAMAN

M is also for ...
MCATEER, Jason
who, unlike former Liverpool pal McManaman, did not leave his beloved Anfield of his own volition. The club chose to accept a £4m bid from Blackburn for the services of the energetic Irish international who left the Melwood training ground in tears after saying his good-byes to his old teammates. More tears followed at Rovers.

PHIL NEVILLE

'THE MAJORITY OF SPURS FANS WEREN'T TOO IMPRESSED WHEN THE CLUB HIRED OLD GOONER GEORGE, BUT I DIDN'T SEE MANY OF THEM COMPLAINING WHEN HE LED SPURS TO WORTHINGTON CUP SUCCESS...AND INTO EUROPE !

ALLAN NIELSEN scores in the Worthington Cup Final at Wembley

O is for ... O'NEILL, MARTIN

who showed that there is some loyalty left in football, after all. The excitable Irishman with a wonderful gift of the gab, was the man Leeds United seriously targeted to be their new boss when George Graham shamelessly walked out on his Elland Road contract to head back to London. O'Neill, flattered by Leeds' interest and no doubt thinking his cash-strapped days as a manager would be over, gave the offer due consideration but the wealth of support from Leicester players and fans alike ultimately won the day. O'Neill turned down the opportunity to go to a bigger club and see out his contract with Leicester; no doubt with a few provisos laid down to his Filbert Street bosses before he did so.

O is also for ... O'LEARY, DAVID

who, unlike Northern Irishman O'Neill, prefers the softly, softly approach to management. At least when he's talking to the media. Early results suggest he gets his points across to his players more than adequately and they have responded brilliantly. He predicted a top four finish and got it, so not a bad judge either.

MARTIN O'NEILL

IT SAYS SOMETHING ABOUT PALLISTER'S CONTRIBUTION TO MAN UNITED'S SUCCESS THAT ALEX FERGUSON FELT THE NEED TO SHELL OUT £10M ON JAAP STAM AS HIS REPLACEMENT !

P is for ... PALLISTER, GARY

whose transfer from Manchester United back to his old club Middlesbrough before the start of last season was remarkable for the fact that he was transferred for exactly the same fee (£2.5m) as he was when he first joined United nine years previous. Not too many players hold their value over such a long period of time, especially when they get into their 30s. But Pally, even with his dodgy back, was well worth investing in as far as his old United teammate Bryan Robson was concerned. Although he missed a few games early on, the former England defender's experience helped settle a rocky ship in danger of sinking at one point.

P is also for ... POYET, GUSTAVO

who is one of the outstanding foreign imports at Stamford Bridge – and let's face it, there are a few. A powerful midfielder who scores important goals, especially with his head, the Uruguayan was sorely missed through injury for a lengthy spell and his absence may well have cost Chelsea the title.

SKY SPORTS

1998 1999

FOOTBALL REVIEW

R is for ... **REID, PETER**
who stuck to his task and his attacking principles last season and was rewarded by his players with a 100-point haul in the First Division to clinch the championship and avoid the dreaded play-offs.

S is for ... **SCHMEICHEL, PETER**
who went through the worst spell of his glorious Manchester United career mid-way through last season when, possibly for the first time in his sporting life, he looked out of sorts and totally disinterested. Fair play then to Alex Ferguson for granting the Great Dane a winter holiday in the Caribbean to rest his aching limbs and the time to sort his head out before returning for one last effort. Schmeichel came back a new man and, having announced he would be quitting the club at the end of the season, vowed to end his career at Old Trafford in style. Back to his awe-inspiring best for the final third of the season, the Danish international played a massive part in United's surge towards the domestic League and Cup double before bringing the curtain down on his trophy-laden, nine-year spell as the club's undisputed number one by lifting the Champions Cup as a fitting stand-in for suspended skipper Roy Keane.

S is also for ... **SHEARER, ALAN**
who suffered the disappointment of a second successive FA Cup Final defeat with Newcastle last season and generally looked thoroughly cheesed off with life at the club he preferred to Manchester United. The look on his face at the end of the latest Wembley walloping suggested he might just be regretting his decision to snub United a tad.

Q is for ...
QUINN, NIALL
who cheered up Peter Reid no end with some towering performances up front for Sunderland as the Wearsiders, so despondent a year before when they lost out in the play-off final to Charlton, made it to the top flight with room to spare this time. Quinn's partnership with the prolific Kevin Phillips was obviously a key factor behind Sunderland's roaring success and when the former Watford striker, a revelation since his transfer a couple of seasons ago, was injured for a spell Quinn shouldered the responsibility brilliantly, and with some ease. The Republic of Ireland international used to be recognised as little more than a beanpole striker who was good in the air. But, as anyone at the Stadium of Light will tell you, there's more to his game than that. Much more. His link-up play, ability to hold the ball up and the quality of many of his goals have served to enhance his reputation.

Q is also for ... **QUAYE, PETER OFORI**
who you may not have heard much about but is apparently being tipped to become the new Ronaldo. The Ghanaian forward has been making a name for himself in Greece with Olympiakos but has been watched by a number of British clubs. Apologies to Nigel Quashie for not using him as our second Q.

R is for ... **ROBSON, BRYAN**
who has continued to put his faith in experience rather than youth as he bids to establish Middlesbrough as a Premiership force to be reckoned with. Certainly, after being relegated from the top flight and returning immediately, Boro made a better job of competing with the elite last season, although their promising start was undermined by a diabolical spell in the middle of the season. Robson is hoping for better things this season, not just from the team as a whole but Paul Gascoigne in particular. Robson has stood by the troubled star through thick and thin (mainly thin) and still believes Gazza has got enough left in the tank to make another impact on the international scene. First he needs to reward his club manager with a season of consistency rather than occasional flashes of brilliance.

ALAN SHEARER

KEVIN KEEGAN SAID BEFORE THE START OF THE CURRENT SEASON THAT THE DOOR IS STILL OPEN FOR GAZZA IF HE GETS HIMSELF IN SHAPE AND IS PERFORMING WELL ON A REGULAR BASIS. IT'S UP TO GAZZA NOW !

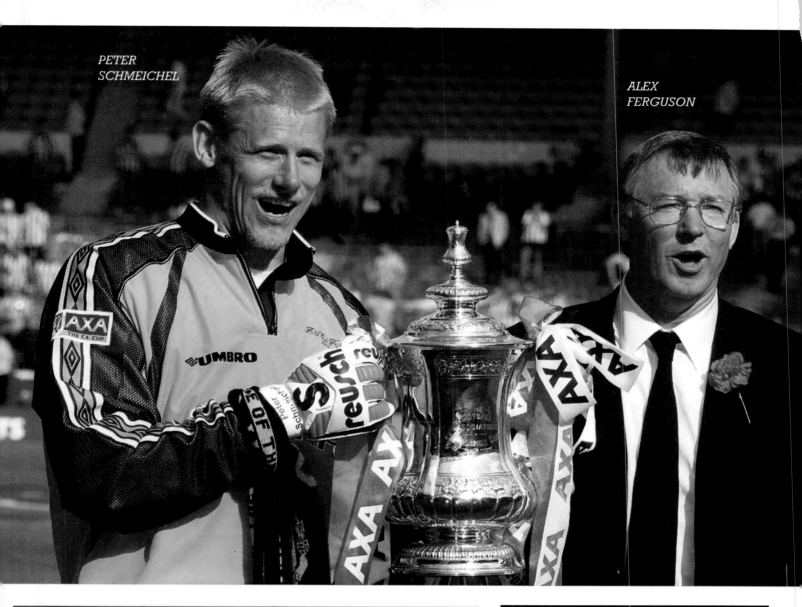

PETER
SCHMEICHEL

ALEX
FERGUSON

WHATEVER YOU THOUGHT OF GRAHAM TAYLOR AS ENGLAND MANAGER YOU CAN ONLY MARVEL AT WHAT HE HAS ACHIEVED WITH SUCH LIMITED RESOURCES AT WATFORD . . . AGAIN !

GRAHAM
TAYLOR

T is for …

TAYLOR, GRAHAM

who has finally shrugged off his international failings and the ridicule which went with it to prove beyond doubt that, rather than vegetating, he has grown in both strength and stature. The 'England thing' will never go away totally, of course, and he still regrets not making a success of 'the best job in football', as he described it. But you have to admire his resolve and ability to bounce back, albeit with more than a little help from Watford chairman Elton John who proudly claims responsibility for luring Taylor back to football, perhaps against his better judgement. Taylor, you may remember, led Watford from the old Fourth Division to the First in the 80s and took the club to the dizzy heights of second place in the top flight. The odds on him doing the same again are so much greater this time around, but stranger things have happened.

T is also for … TODD, COLIN

who could only stand back and watch with admiration and envy as canny old fox Graham Taylor rallied his Watford troops and condemned Bolton, arguably the better footballing side over the season, to another year in the First Division. To Todd's credit, he was typically gracious in defeat…as ever.

SKY SPORTS

1998 1999

FOOTBALL REVIEW

PIERRE VAN HOOIJDONK

U **is for ... UNSWORTH, DAVID**

who simply couldn't decide where he wanted to play his football before the start of last season. Contracted to West Ham but unhappy living in the south, the former Everton defender felt that a move to the West Midlands and Aston Villa would provide a cure for his homesickness. But within days, and without kicking a ball for his new club, he announced he was still too far away from his native Merseyside and that the chance of a return to his old club Everton was simply too tempting to refuse. Naturally, Villa were a little miffed by Unsworth's fickle fancies but at least the powerhouse defender's swift departure gave young England star Gareth Barry the chance to impress at the top level. And boy, did he impress as Villa raced to the top of the table only to fade when the going got tough. As for Unsworth and Everton, well...

V **is for ... VAN HOOIJDONK, PIERRE**

who many people felt should have been kicked out of English football altogether after refusing to return to Nottingham Forest in time for the start of last season. The dissenting Dutchman, despite scoring the goals which fired Forest back to the Premiership, was disappointed that the club had failed to strengthen the squad to his liking and he basically described his teammates as a bunch of no-hopers. Needless to say, without Van Hooijdonk and his old strike partner Kevin Campbell, who was sold to Trabzonspor in Turkey, Forest struggled from day one and were ultimately relegated at the end of a truly miserable season. It could be argued that the Dutch international was correct in his assessment of the club's chances, but his actions did nothing to help the cause and when he did eventually return under protest his performances lacked conviction and smacked of a player who wanted to get away. Finally he did, by signing for Vitesse Arnhem in a £3.5m deal in the summer.

WHAT PIERRE DID WAS BOTH SELFISH AND GREEDY, NOT TO MENTION DISRESPECTFUL TO BOTH THE TEAMMATES HE CRITICISED AND THE FANS WHO HE FAILED TO REMEMBER PAY HIS WAGES !

W is for ...WALLACE, Rod

who surprised a lot of people before the start of last season when he turned down the offer of a new contract with Leeds to take up the option of a free transfer under the Bosman ruling and joined Glasgow Rangers. But with three medals in the cabinet by the end of his first year with the Glasgow giants, who's questioning his decision now? Certainly not Rodney himself who described the thrill of winning the treble north of the border as 'the greatest moment of my career'. With 'Super Ally' McCoist calling time on his prolific Rangers' career and opting for a swansong with Kilmarnock, the Ibrox faithful were desperate for a new goal hero, and they found him in the diminutive shape of Wallace who plundered 26 goals in all competitions as Rangers swept all before them. He still finished 12 goals behind leading scorer Henrik Larsson of Celtic, but who gives a stuff?

X is for ...X-PROFESSIONAL

footballers who have taken up careers in television after retiring from the game, notably Sky's very own Andy Gray who dabbled in management as number two at Aston Villa and was offered the 'big one' at his old club Everton before deciding a safer future lay in TV. Andy's in good company on the Skysports' pay roll with the likes of Rodney Marsh, Clive Allen, George Best and Frank McLintock amongst the impressive line-up of guest analysts whose forthright views make them popular and respected members of the Sky team. Not too sure about the footballing ability of Richard Keys and Martin Tyler though!

DWIGHT YORKE

> IN MY VIEW DWIGHT YORKE HAS HAD A BIGGER INFLUENCE AT UNITED THAN 'KING ERIC' BECAUSE HE DID IT IN BIG EUROPEAN GAMES WHEREAS CANTONA DIDN'T. HOW DWIGHT WASN'T NAMED PLAYER OF THE YEAR I'LL NEVER KNOW !

Y is for ... YORKE, Dwight

who realised within weeks of his £12.6m move to Old Trafford that he was made for Manchester United. Alex Ferguson's bold decision to shell out so much on a single player – so soon after spending £10m on defender Jaap Stam – was questioned but, after all this time, we should have known better. Fergie hasn't boobed too many times in the transfer market, and it soon transpired he had staged another massive transfer coup. Not only did Yorke produce 29 goals of his own but his mere presence, and that flashing smile, also brought the best out of Fergie's other big-money striker Andy Cole who struck up an instant understanding with the former Aston Villa striker. What must have pleased the United boss more than anything about his shrewd investment was that Yorke produced goals in games when it really mattered; finding the target no fewer than eight times during the club's magnificent Champions League campaign. A treble winner in his first season; not bad eh?

Z is for ... ZIDANE, Zinedine

who is one of few players we can think of whose surname begins with Z. He's certainly the only one whose christian name begins with Z too. Bet he's last in the phone book! Seriously though Zidane deserves a mention for being named the World Footballer of the Year after inspiring France to World Cup success on their own soil in 1998. Okay, so his performances for Italian club Juventus last season perhaps didn't live up to his virtuoso displays for his country but there is no disputing that Zidane is one of the game's great natural talents. Injuries didn't help his or Juve's cause and it was with some embarrassment that the proud Italian club was forced to attempt European qualification via the Intertoto Cup.

TOP 10 LISTS

AND WE THOUGHT RUGBY PLAYERS WERE HARD!

Ten Rugby League players whose names bely their business ...

1 Les KISS (London coach)
2 Paul NEWLOVE (St Helens)
3 Stuart SPRUCE (Bradford)
4 Deon BIRD (Gateshead)
5 Jason FLOWERS (Castleford)
6 Aaron RAPER (Castleford)
7 Richard GAY (Castleford)
8 Gael TALLEC (Castleford)
9 David MAIDEN (Gateshead)
10 Nick PINKNEY (Halifax)

ARE YOU SURE YOU WANTED TO SAY THAT?
Ten contenders for sport's 'Foot in Mouth' award

1) **'There's going to be a real ding-dong when the bell goes'** (David Coleman)
2) **'The lead car is absolutely unique, except for the one behind it which is identical'** (Murray Walker)
3) **'I can see the carrot at the end of the tunnel'** (Stuart Pearce)
4) **'I owe a lot to my parents, especially my mother and father'** (Greg Norman)
5) **'Playing with wingers is more effective against European sides like Brazil than English sides like Wales'** (Ron Greenwood)
6) **'Sure there have been injuries and deaths in boxing - but none of them serious'** (Alan Minter)
7) **'The racecourse is as level as a billiard ball'** (Johnny Francome)
8) **'Watch the time -it gives you an indication of how fast they are running'** (Ron Pickering)
9) **'That's inches away from being millimetre perfect'** (Ted Lowe)
10) **'If history repeats itself, I should think we can expect the same thing again'** (Terry Venables)

GO ON LADS, GIVE US A SONG!

Ten dance records from '99 which may have been dedicated to the following ...

1 **HEY BOY, HEY GIRL** – David Beckham and Posh Spice
2 **GOT MYSELF TOGETHER** – Stan Collymore
3 **HAPPINESS HAPPENING** – Sir Alex Ferguson
4 **THAT DON'T IMPRESS ME MUCH** – Alex Ferguson to Joe Royle
5 **OOH LA LA** - Frank Lebouef and Dennis Wise Guy
6 **SCAR TISSUE** – Darren Anderton
7 **PICK A PART THAT'S NEW** – Darren Anderton
8 **SWEAR IT AGAIN** – Gordon Strachan
9 **PERFECT MOMENT** – Man United squad '99
10 **WRIGHT HERE, WRIGHT NOW** – Fat Boy Ian

COMING UP NEXT:

SENSATIONAL SKY SPORTS POSTER SECTION FEATURING TOP QUALITY PIX OF THE FOLLOWING: ANNA KORNIKOVA, DAVID GINOLA, MIKA HAKKINEN, TIGER WOODS, LEEDS RHINOS AND OTHERS ...

Treble Shooters!

Glasgow Rangers

Martina Hingis

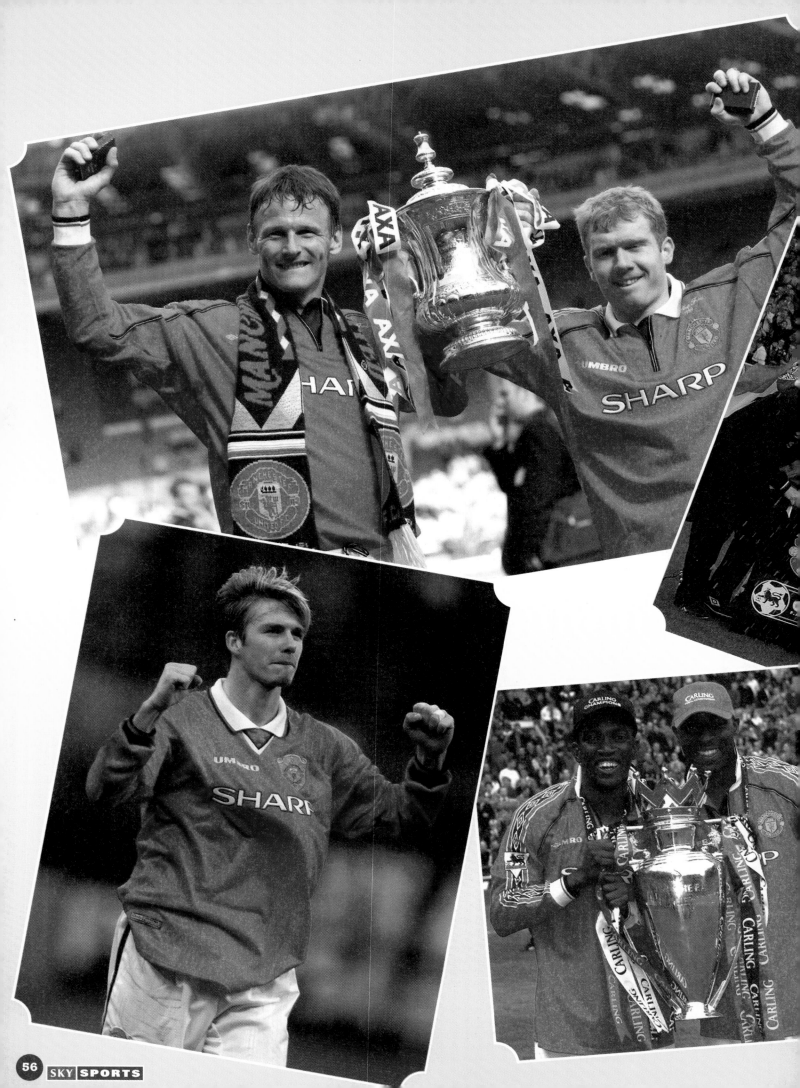

Manchester United

Treble Shooters!

CARLING CHAMPIONS 1998-99

CARLING CHAMPIONS 1998-99

SOLSKJÆR 20

Wizards of Oz

David Ginola

Anna Kournikova

TOP 10 LISTS

TEN FOOTBALLERS WITH ALTERNATIVE CAREERS:

GIZZA JOB MATE...

1. MARK DRAPER
2. JIMMY HASSELBAINK MANAGER
3. IAN TAYLOR
4. STEPHEN CARR SALESMAN
5. COLIN COOPER
6. GARY CROFTER
7. BEN THATCHER
8. RIGOBERT SONG WRITER
9. CARL TILER
10. CRAIG FORREST RANGER

NOT IN A MONTH OF SUNDAYS ...

Ten things you wouldn't catch a commentator saying

1. 'There's Alex Ferguson, the first to shake the referee's hand once again'
2. 'And once more Damon Hill leads his rivals into the first bend'
3. 'That was solid England batting all the way down to number ten'
4. 'Carl Fogarty must surely be regretting his decision to ditch Honda'
5. 'Nick Faldo has decided it's time to stop tampering with his swing'
6. 'Lawrence Dallaglio is back with his credibility in tact'
7. 'Anna Kournikova looks a bit rough today'
8. 'Dennis Bergkamp, Arsenal's Champions League hero in Athens
9. 'The lithe, athletic figure of Shane Warne begins his run-up'
10. 'There's Colin Montgomerie laughing and joking with the crowd'

ANYONE FOR SCRABBLE?

Ten sporting stars whose names would make great scores in a game of Scrabble (if you could actually get them on the board) ...

1. FABRIZIO RAVANELLI - ITALIAN FOOTBALLER
2. FUZZY ZOELLER - AMERICAN GOLFER
3. ANNA KOURNIKOVA - RUSSIAN TENNIS PLAYER
4. ANDONI ZUBIZARETTA - FORMER SPANISH GOALKEEPER
5. JACQUES VILLENEUVE - MOTOR RACING DRIVER
6. MARK PHILLIPOUSSIS - AUSSIE TENNIS PLAYER
7. KONSTANTINOS KARTEROULIOTIS - GREEK FOOTBALLER
8. SANATH JAYASURIYA - SRI LANKAN CRICKETER
9. TEMIOURAZ KIKLEIDZE - GEORGIAN BOXER
10. HEINZ-HARALD FRENTZEN - MOTOR RACING DRIVER

COMING UP NEXT:

RUGBY UNION TAKES CENTRE STAGE AS WE TALK TO THE ENGLAND CAPTAIN AND THE YOUNG STAR THEY SAY IS THE MICHAEL OWEN OF THE OVAL BALL GAME ...

SKY SPORTS

RUGBY UNION REVIEW

CAPTAIN FANTASTIC!

Captain of Allied Dunbar Premiership champions Leicester; Premiership Player Of The Year, Daily Telegraph Readers' Player Of The Year and The RFU Player Of The Year. Not a bad season for Leicester and England legend Martin Johnson. Oh yes, and he was made captain of his country as well ...

The plaudits we have just mentioned, and there have been many others throughout a distinguished career, are just as much the result of hard work and dedication as they are for Johnson's supreme forward skills. But he is not one to gloat about his own personal achievements; he much prefers to talk about 'the team'.

"I thought that we (Leicester) had been a bit ragged at times in the previous season and it was vital that we pulled the squad together, maintained our discipline and worked as a unit," said the England man whose club side won the Allied Dunbar Premiership title almost at a canter.

"We had a great team spirit all the way through the season and our management team of Dean Richards and John Wells must take a lot of the credit for that." See what we mean about the importance he attaches to 'the team'.

But wasn't it difficult to have two former team-mates in charge?

"To a certain extent, yes. We knew that having to deal with Dean and John as players one minute and as the management the next might well have been difficult for both sides, but the transition was a lot smoother than we might have dared to hope for and I was pleasantly surprised by that.

"Deano in particular was definitely one of the boys in the dressing room. He loved all the chat and the banter and in fact when he first took over the running of the side, he still insisted on getting changed in the same dressing room as the rest of us.

"I wasnt so sure that that was such a good idea, so we changed that around, but apart from that I haven't noticed anything too different. Of course both Deano and John have left no-one in any doubt that they will have the last word if there are any tricky issues to be sorted out, but there have been surprisingly few problems."

If only things had gone as smoothly for the national side. Off the pitch the Lawrence Dallaglio incident cast a long shadow, while on the field the loss of the Five Nations to Scotland after a last-gasp Wembley defeat at the hands of Wales was an unexpected shock to the system for an England side that hadn't really sparked during the tournament, but which had never really looked in any serious danger of letting the title slip from its grasp. When it did the critics had a field day, of course. Not that Johnno was unduly worried.

"During the Wales game we actually played some of our best rugby of the tournament," he argues. "The mistake that we made was that when we were two tries to nil up and seriously on top, we didn't kill them off. Losing right at the death was very disappointing, of course, and you have to be critical of some of the things that happened.

"In the first half Wales never looked like scoring a try, yet still managed to put 18 points on the board; all of them from 30 metres plus out. Giving penalties away on the line when you're defending for your life and under immense pressure is one thing, but to concede so many that far out is criminal.

"I'd have to say that some of the refereeing decisions were a bit harsh, but even so ... we really should have killed that game off. We had plenty of chances in the second half, but we didn't score a try. We made numerous breaks, but we didn't finish them off."

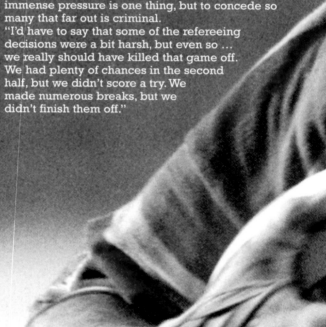

PREPARING FOR THE WORLD CUP

By the time many of you read this, England and their skipper will know their World Cup fate. But whether the feelings at the end of it all are ones of despair or delight, you can rest assured that under Johnson's leadership there will be no lack of effort.

Johnson was utterly dismissive of the idea that the defeat by Wales, as disappointing as it was, would have a significant impact on England's World Cup build-up. "That's just not how the players look at things. I don't play for England thinking about it being a build-up for the World Cup. I don't even think about the next game. Whatever game I'm playing, well that's the game I'm playing. I don't do anything except try to win the game for England," says the skipper.

"People were talking about the build-up to the World Cup for three years beforehand and that's ridiculous. In '95 we beat the French at Twickenham quite convincingly and they played poorly. Yet they ended up being an inch off getting to the World Cup Final.

"England got thrashed in '91 by 40 points to 15 against Australia and yet made it to the World Cup final. So what does all that say? I believe you can play poorly right up to October and still win the World Cup, because the World Cup is different.

"I just give my best every game, because in every game I play my place is on the line. If I started thinking to myself 'I'm looking towards the World Cup so I don1t have to do much in this match' then the only thing that's certain is that I'll end up watching it on the telly!"

JOHNSON:
The stats
Club: **Leicester**
Position: **Lock**
Date of Birth: **9 March, 1970**
Place of Birth: **Solihull**
Height: **6' 6"**
Weight: **18st 7lbs**
England/Lions Apps: **45**
Test Tries/Points: **1/5**

Stats up to June 1

THE DALLAGLIO AFFAIR

Rugby Union internationals expect to take a few whacks in the line of duty, but no-one in the history of the game suffered more than former Engand captain Lawrence Dallaglio last May.

Dallaglio stood down even before the RFU investigation into News of the World allegations about drug taking and dealing. And almost unnoticed amongst all the fuss and palaver, the England captaincy was handed over to Leicester lock Martin Johnson.

His initial reaction. Nothing at all, of course. Not until the official press conference a couple of days later, anyway. 'Johnno', as many frustrated rugby writers will tell you, isn't a great fan of the press.

And given what his teammate Dallaglio had to put up with, it's not all that surprising, is it? "I feel very sorry for Lawrence as a team-mate and as a bloke," the latest England skipper told us. "He was missed in the months after all this blew up. But as a professional all I could do was carry on and do my best for England.

"They weren't the circumstances that I would have wanted to be given the England captaincy under, but what's done is done and all the players could do was focus on the tasks at hand and prepare ourselves for the World Cup as professionally and thoroughly as we could.

"We had to carry on as if none of this had happened."

SKY SPORTS
RUGBY UNION REVIEW

THE STORY SO FAR ...

Jonathan Peter Wilkinson went to Lord Wandsworth College and started playing rugby at four (or so they claim at Farnham RFC in Hampshire). He was spotted by Newcastle at 16 and regularly drove two hours to Bristol where David Aldred, the former Minnesota Vikings kicker, put him through his paces. Aldred, now part of the England set up, recalls: "I started with Jonny at the age of 16. But by then he could already hit the ball. He's got fantastically supportive parents, without being pushy – and that's important. He was identified as someone who was going to be special by Newcastle, even then. I started working with him at the Bristol University fields behind my house. What was important was that he had the desire to want to make the effort. It's not just kicking at the posts. Now Jonny has got to be among the top echelon of the players I've coached, certainly in terms of application and commitment.
"He's up there with Rob Andrew, Neil Jenkins and David Campese, who I helped for a while. And remember, a kicker reaches his peak just before he's mentally had enough. Obviously we've yet to see the best of Jonny Wilkinson."

WILKO'S PURR-FECT, SAYS CATT

Mike Catt, England's South African-born fly-half, has nothing but praise for the Newcastle sensation and says: "Wilko has been great since he came into the side. He's kicked well and been very solid in defence. In fact, there's a whole wave of young talent coming through with Wilko and that can only be good for England. I certainly don't mind the competition.
"If you look at the average age of our back line now it's really young as long as Jeremy Guscott doesn't make a comeback! But seriously, if these lads like Steve Hanley, Dan Luger and Wilko are good enough for the Five Nations then they're good enough for the World Cup I think a lot of this new talent is down to the improvement in our Premiership. With all the Southern Hemisphere players passing on their experiences, our youngsters are getting the kind of grounding in the game which I had as a youngster in Port Elizabeth. In South Africa, rugby is everything. A religion. And that's what is happening now for young English players. Pat Lam at Northampton and Francois Pienaar at Saracens can only help the young guys coming through. Wilko is certainly a good example of that at Newcastle. He'll be one of the greats."

JONNY ON THE SPOT

Whether he likes it or not England's brilliant young fly half Jonny Wilkinson has been saddled with the title of the 'Michael Owen of Rugby Union' and so far the impact he has made at international level has been every bit as great as that of Liverpool's footballing sensation. Owen, of course, earned worldwide acclaim for his performances at France '98 and so, in Rugby World Cup year, we decided to put Jonny on the spot in this special Q&A...

Q   Jonny, you missed just two kicks out of 21 during the Five Nations, but how disappointing was it to lose the title in such dramatic circumstances against Wales?
A   It was very, VERY disappointing. I just hope that some day I get the chance to play at Wembley again, preferably against Wales. Of course, I was proud of my kicking record but it didn't mean as much as it would have done had we beaten the Welsh and won the championship.

Q   We understand that you were only four when you first started playing rugby, but how old were you when you set your heart on a career in Union?
A   I guess I was around eight. All the other kids in my class wanted to do the usual stuff like drive trains and become astronauts. I wanted to play rugby for England. I'm very proud to be able to say I have achieved that ambition. Now I want to stay in the England team.

Q   You made such an incredible impact at the highest level, and for your club side Newcastle, but what other ambitions do you have?
A   I want to help England stop finishing up second best to the Southern Hemisphere nations. That's got to change and I think it will. I'd also like to become known as a great back possessing all the attributes. Kicking's very important but I've got to work on other aspects of my game.

Q   As a near-perfect kicker experts say you should be at the fulcrum of the team, wearing the No 10 jersey at fly-half. But where do you prefer to play?
A   I'm drifting away from stand-off because I've been playing so much at centre. You can't just move back into a role you haven't played for a while, especially fly half where the team's weight seems to be on your shoulders. You need loads of games in that position before you can even begin to make your mark.

Q   What do you think about suggestions from admirers that you are as near to the perfect kicker as there is in the game at the present time?
A   It's nice of them to say, but I don't agree. I'm desperate to find out the reason why I still kick the odd ball badly. Why can't I get it right every time? I've considered doing a part-time course in sports-related psychology to find out how I can improve my mindset to cut out errors.

Q   How much potential do you think the England squad, which has been carefully developed by Clive Woodward, possesses - and how far can you go?
A   I said before the World Cup that there was absolutely no reason why we could not win it and then stay at the top of international rugby for years to come. We have promised so much for so long and gone so close to achieving it. Young players are coming through who can be around for a very long time.

Q   In his search for the 'perfect mixture' Clive Woodward has not been afraid to give youth a chance, do you see that trend continuing?
A   As far as I'm concerned the more youngsters given the chance the better. I may be biased but I think the addition of youth adds extra excitement and buzz to the squad. The older players look at us and it spurs them on to try and keep us out the side. It improves competition for places and benefits everyone concerned.

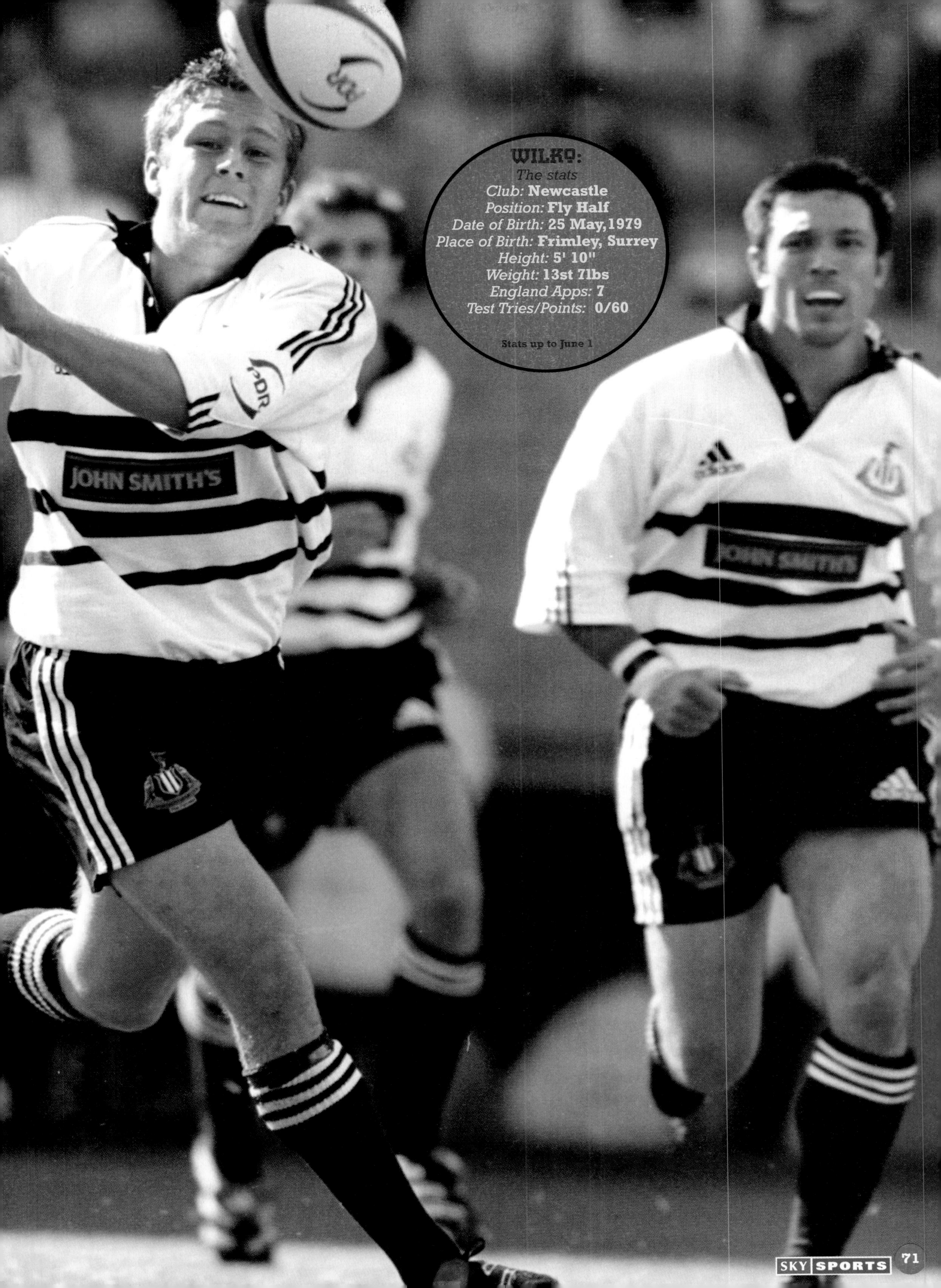

WILKO:
The stats
Club: **Newcastle**
Position: **Fly Half**
Date of Birth: **25 May, 1979**
Place of Birth: **Frimley, Surrey**
Height: **5' 10"**
Weight: **13st 7lbs**
England Apps: **7**
Test Tries/Points: **0/60**

Stats up to June 1

SKY SPORTS

in conjunction with

THE Sun

WIN!

A DAY AT A TOP SPORTS EVENT AS A SUN REPORTER!

HOLD THE BACK PAGE

The makers of the Sky Sports annual have joined forces with our friends at the Sun, the country's biggest-selling daily newspaper, to bring you a unique competition – which is both entertaining and rewarding.

The Sun's headline writers are among the best in the business, especially when it comes to selling sports stories in their punchy, clever and witty way.

We've selected half a dozen headlines from some of the major stories which have unfolded this year and all you have to do is work out 'the tale behind the title'.

Select three of the six headlines you feel you are sure about and in each

case write the story behind the headline. The first person pulled out of the hat with three correct story lines to their name will win a fabulous day out at a top sporting event in this country, hired for the day as a Sun reporter.

A professional journalist will accompany you to the game/tournament/event which you select and will watch from the Press box before witnessing the press conferences with the coaches or sportsmen concerned. You will also be asked to compile your own story from the day, including your observations and the reactions of the stars, and your story will appear in the Sun newspaper at an appropriate time.

Can You Tell The Tale Behind The [   ] Headline?

TENNIS
Brit's gonna be our year
Story:_____
_____
_____
_____
_____

FOOTBALL
BRAVEST REF IN BRITAIN!
Story:_____
_____
_____
_____

SUPERBIKES
FOGGY 1 VIALLI 0
Story:_____
_____
_____
_____

RUGBY UNION
I'LL STAND BY MY MAN
Coach Woodward backing Dallaglio
Story:_____
_____
_____
_____

CRICKET
OLONGA MAKES IT SOLONGA INDIA!
Story:_____
_____
_____

FOOTBALL
FINAL WHISTLES
BLACK 'N' WHITE ARMANI
Story:_____
_____
_____

There was hardly a dry eye in the house when Jose Maria Olazabal helped himself to his second, yet by far his most rewarding, US Masters title at Augusta this year. Even the most patriotic American supporters were choking back tears as the genial Spaniard affectionately known as 'Olly' overcame a career threatening injury – and the deep depression which went with it – to record one of the most popular golfing victories for years. "I was so proud of myself," admitted Olazabal as he slid comfortably into his green jacket. And why not? After spending 18 months out of the game suffering with chronic pain from the joints in his feet which reduced him to a crawling recluse at times, 'Olly' feared he may never walk properly again, let alone swing a club in anger. But those days of dark despair were well and truly behind him as he repeated his 1994 Augusta success to complete one of sports great comebacks....

OLLY GOOD SHOW!

Comeback king Olazabal is still the Master !

LITTLE MORE THAN TWO YEARS AGO I HAD DOUBTS NOT JUST ABOUT MY GOLF CAREER BUT MY WHOLE QUALITY OF LIFE. I WANT TO THANK ALL MY FAMILY AND FRIENDS FOR THEIR INCREDIBLE SUPPORT!

I REMEMBER READING THINGS WHILE I WAS AWAY FROM THE GAME THAT WERE SO SILLY, LIKE I HAD AIDS, OR I WAS HIDING AWAY BECAUSE I WAS SO FAT. THOSE THINGS WERE BOTH STUPID AND HURTFUL!

OLLY FACT
He spent 18 months away from the game fearing for his career before a German specialist traced the problem with his feet to a trapped nerve and set him on the road to recovery.

THE FIRST PERSON WHO RANG ME AFTER THE MASTERS WAS THE KING OF SPAIN. HE WAS IN A MEETING WITH SOME BISHOPS BUT SAID HE MANAGED TO ESCAPE FOR A SHORT WHILE TO CONGRATULATE ME!

OLLY FACT
Olazabal's victory in the 1999 Masters was the 11th by a European player at Augusta in the last 20 years, and his second in the last six.

OLLY FACT
His back nine in the final round at Augusta this year was described by some as 'the finest nine holes in the 53-year history of the tournament'.

WE REALLY DON'T KNOW OUR LIMITS UNTIL WE ARE FACED WITH SOMETHING AS BAD I WENT THROUGH. IT WAS A VERY DIFFICULT TIME FOR ME AND MY FAMILY!

OLLY FACT

33-year-old 'Olly' still lives at home with his parents and sister in the tiny fishing village of Fuenterrabia in northern Spain, although he has his own 'section' within a big house.

NEW KING OF SPAIN

Seve Ballesteros started the Spanish golfing revolution; Jose Maria Olazabal has brilliantly carried on the mantle; and now there's a new kid on the block ready to keep his country at the forefront of the sport in the new century.

Sergio Garcia, the 1998 Amateur champion who also finished as the low amateur at the 1999 Masters, has already taken great strides on the professional circuit and appears to be the natural successor to his famous, fellow countrymen.

He did his growing reputation no harm whatsoever when he finished ahead of the likes of Tiger Woods, Fred Couples and Justin Leonard on his US tour debut, claiming an impressive third place in the Byron Nelson Classic in Texas earlier in the year.

It was an eye-catching performance by the teenager from Valencia, who caused many senior pros to sit up and take notice of his wonderful, natural talent. Not least Europe's Ryder Cup captain Mark James who said: "I have been very impressed by what Sergio has achieved.

"He may only have turned pro after the Masters but he has been playing almost full time on our Tour for virtually three years as an amateur. And he has more than held his own - the British Open aside."

Garcia, the youngest ever winner of the European Amateur Championship at 15, also won the British Amateur title in 1998 a year after claiming his first professional victory in the 1997 Catalan Open; one of more than 70 tournaments he has won in ten different countries.

He says he owes much of his early success to 'my second father' Ballesteros who returns the compliment by saying: "Sergio is the best player I have ever seen at his age. He has everything a champion needs.

"He is a great ball striker, he is good under pressure and he has excellent concentration. But, above all, he has great passion for the game. He practices hard and loves to be a winner."

Tiger Woods, a teenage sensation himself not so long ago, was also glowing in his praise of the young Spanish star who threatens to challenge the American for the major honours for years to come. Tiger says: "I wasn't as talented as him at 19. He has the right attitude and WILL be successful."

OTHER COMEBACK KINGS

John Elway – American Football
Monica Seles – Tennis
Jona Lomu – Rugby Union
Joe Bugner – Boxing
Diego Maradona – Football
Shane Warne – Cricket
Andre Agassi – Tennis
Steve Redgrave - Rowing

GOLF
REVIEW

KNEES-UP FOR PAYNE STEWART AT US OPEN

Payne Stewart dedicated his second Open success to his late father and his devoted wife after clinching the title with a sensational 15-foot putt on the last hole at Pinehurst.

It was the memory of dad, together with a putting tip from wife Tracy following the penultimate round, which combined to inspire Stewart as he went head-to-head with brilliant left-hander Phil Mickelson. The eventual winner went to the first tee emotionally charged up after watching a television clip about him and his father, who taught him the game but saw him win only one professional tournament before he died.

"I stood there and bawled in front of the TV," said Stewart who watched the short feature at the start of the broadcast coverage of the Open's final day…ironically on Father's Day. "I cried and thought a lot about my father and I probably got a lot of strength from that. And then I came to the golf course."

The fired-up American wasted no time as he birdied the first hole by sinking a 15-foot putt and then led the championship for most of the day before he faltered slightly as the pressure mounted towards the end."

It was then his putting prowess pulled him through as he one-putted the last three holes to overtake Mickelson and win his second Open and third major championship.

Stewart, who admits that his putting does let him down at times, said his wife had given him a tip on the Saturday night and that by following her brief he succeeded in taking only 24 putts on the Sunday.

Tracy had noticed that Payne seemed to be moving his head slightly when he stroked the ball. "She said you're wanting to see it go in before it goes in," he recalled. "So I went out onto the practice green that night and I worked on it. I putted with my eyes closed; I never looked up. And I took that out on the golf course the next day. I never moved my head to watch a putt." The rest, of course, is history…

KNICKERBOCKER GLORY

CROSS DRESSERS!

stars take a leaf out of poser Payne's fashion book

Dapper dresser Payne Stewart has become one of the most well-known faces on the PGA Tour in recent years – and not just for producing the sort of inspired golf which saw him win the US Open under the severest pressure in June. He has also become the most instantly recognisable figure on the circuit because of his trademark style of dress; a throw-back to the good, old days with his plus-fours, eye-catching socks and natty choice of head gear.

Stewart's snazzy attire often reflects the colours sported by some of the country's American Football teams, usually those of NFL teams who play in the area where a particular golf tournament is taking place. Always a winner with the locals.

With the Open champion preferring the more traditional golfing glad-rags, we wondered what other international sports' stars would look like in kit or clobber from a bygone era ... like David Beckham (above.)

Plus we check out how some of them would shape up in the uniforms of their modern-day counterparts from other sports...

ARE YOU A SKY SPORTS SUPERBRAIN?

CRYPTIC QUIZ

Solve the following clues to work out the names of these top stars from the worlds of football, rugby union, rugby league, cricket and golf...

1. This footballer was on fire when he scored the goal which clinched the 1999 Premiership trophy for his side.
2. England's rugby union scrum half was really motoring after serving a lengthy ban for stamping?
3. The London Broncos' boss was in a pickle after his team lost the Rugby League Challenge Cup Final at Wembley.
4. No shining armour and no World Cup batting appearances for England during the cricket World Cup in the summer.
5. 1999 was hardly a blooming success for this young English golfing hopeful.

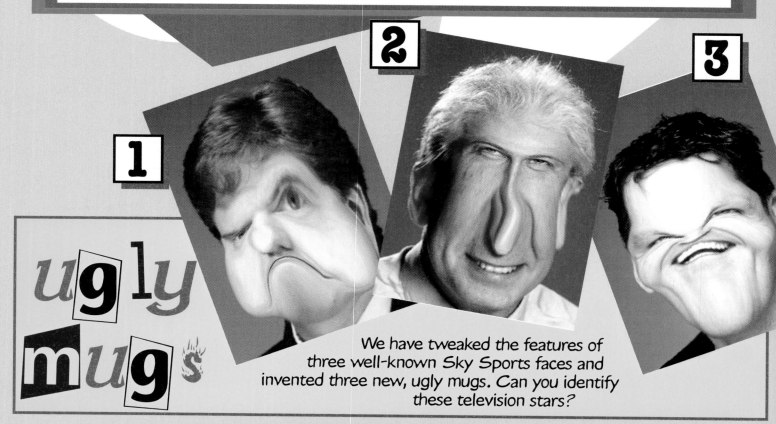

ugly mugs

We have tweaked the features of three well-known Sky Sports faces and invented three new, ugly mugs. Can you identify these television stars?

satellite stars

We have mixed up the names of five well-know sporting celebrities. Solve the anagrams to reveal the stars ...

a) **WASHER ANNE** (Cricket)
b) **HI, I STING AN ARM** (Tennis)
c) **OXEN'S WELL IN** (Boxing)
d) **NO GERM RANG** (Golf)
e) **SARAH LEANER** (Football)

Missing Names

Using the two words shown in each case as a clue fit the name of a well known player in the middle to form two popular phrases (see example). Remember, the spellings are not always correct.

1. DIAMOND **WHITE** LIGHTNING *(snooker)*
2. BOER _____ TORN *(cricket)*
3. GRIZZLY _____ APPLE *(football)*
4. AFTER _____ SIDE *(Sky TV)*
5. STORMIN' _____ CONQUEST *(golf)*

WORDSEARCH

Hidden within the grid below are the names of 10 major sporting events/tournaments which take place around the world. How many can you find and do you know which sports are involved?

```
G W I M B L E D O N P T
R E O C H G I Q R O O T
A Y M X G N J X S U L O
N E P T H E D E R B Y L
D M H W L P K D Y S M M
P I C S A E E N E C P N
R L E L F F Y H I A I D
I K K K R S S R G R C G
X R C A N A M I H L S F
D A N N E P O E H T E A
G C W H R O R S I L R C
E E T I W O R L D C U P
```

Andy's Brainteaser

1. Which Rugby League team is known as the Blue Sox?

2. Who replaced disgraced Lawrence Dallaglio as England Rugby Union captain?

3. Which England player won his 50th cap in the 0-0 draw with Sweden in June?

ANSWERS ON PAGE 83

COMING UP NEXT:

SKY SPORTS **AMERICAN FOOTBALL**

CHECK OUT THE WORLD OF GRIDIRON AS WE PAY TRIBUTE TO A LEGEND

NFLREVIEW

FAREWELL TO A LIVING LEGEND!

16
IS E
FOR N
JOH

Imagine Manchester United losing not only Peter Schmeichel, but Ryan Giggs too. Then pretend that Roy Keane and David Beckham had hung up their boots in sympathy. Now you've got an idea what the retirement of quarterback John Elway, the man who masterminded victories in the last two Super Bowls, means to the Denver Broncos and to American football in general. Elway, who played the game of his life in what would prove to be his final appearance for Denver in last January's Super Bowl XXXIII demolition of the New York Giants, finally quit in May after four months of soul-searching, announcing: "This is really hard for me to say but I can't do it physically anymore."

But the 38-year-old veteran, battered and bruised by 16 gruelling NFL campaigns and a victim of hamstring, rib and back injuries in his last season, left one hell of a legacy. Only two players in gridiron history have ever delivered more touchdown passes, and only one has thrown more total passing yards. No-one else has led a team to more wins. Like Michael Jordan and Wayne Gretsky, the legends of basketball and ice hockey who also retired in 1999, Elway has insisted there is no chance of a comeback. And that is truly ironic, because those were his speciality. He led the Broncos from behind in the final quarter of games or in sudden-death extra time on a staggering 47 occasions.

This true survivor even managed to rebound when his first three trips to the Super Bowl ended in crushing defeats by a combined score of 136-40 and the Broncos became laughing stocks in America. Good news for the rest of the NFL.

While Elway's departure is bad news for the Denver faithful, it could well prove beneficial to the NFL as a whole because the Broncos dominated the 1998/99 campaign from start to finish.

And while the presence of stars like powerful running back Terrell Davis means they will still be a threat this time around, the chasing pack, which features familiar names like the Dallas Cowboys, Miami Dolphins, San Francisco 49ers and Green Bay Packers, is licking its lips.

While the likes of Miami's Dan Marino and San Francisco's Jerry Rice still remain, there is a feeling that it is finally time for a new crop of superstars to emerge.

Look out for two flashy wide receivers, the Jets' Keyshawn Johnson and the Minnesota Vikings' Randy Moss, to be among them, with both players' teams also legitimate Super Bowl candidates. Elsewhere in the NFL there was another goodbye of sorts as

the Houston Oilers' move to Nashville, conducted at the start of the 1998/99 season, was rubber-stamped when the team changed its name to the Tennessee Titans. But the 1999 campaign also sees the return of an old friend as the Cleveland Browns get back to business with an entirely new squad and backroom staff, four years after the old outfit upped sticks to Baltimore and became the Ravens.

EARS
PUGH
STAR
ELWAY

riddell

THE EUROPEAN SCENE

There was a sad farewell in the NFL's European league too, which began its 1999 season without the London Monarchs, the team which once packed over 60,000 fans into Wembley. Put into cold storage by league chiefs after a disastrous 1998 campaign both on and off the park, the 1991 World Bowl winners were replaced by Berlin Thunder, leaving the Scottish Claymores as Britain's sole representatives. Led by quarterback Dameyune Craig, on loan from the NFL's

Carolina Panthers, the Murrayfield and Hampden Park-based outfit couldn't repeat their 1996 feat of becoming champions. But despite a disappointing season for the club, Craig did manage to write himself a piece of American football history.
As the Claymores beat Frankfurt Galaxy on May 22nd, he completed 611 yards' worth of passes - not only further than any NFL Europe player had thrown before, but further than any of the NFL superstars, Elway included, had ever managed. The achievement was ranked so special that the helmet and shirt Craig wore on the

night, together with one of the balls with which he set the record, are now on display in the Pro Football Hall Of Fame in Ohio, usually reserved for the greats of the game.
Breaking records didn't do Craig any harm with the Panthers either, with coach George Seifert, twice a Super Bowl winner as boss of the San Francisco 49ers, saying: "We're very proud. He's done a lot to capture the imagination of fans in Carolina." And maybe, just maybe, as the NFL looks for new stars to follow Elway, Scotland's Braveheart will be among them.

SKY SPORTS

CROSSWORD 2

CLUES ACROSS:

2   Carl Fogarty's great Super Bikes' rival (6)
5   Famous park in Cardiff (4)
8   Affectionate name of golfer Jose-Maria (4)
9   24-hour race in France (2,4)
10 Batsmen tend to get nervous when they reach this figure (6)
12 Where rugby players lock horns (5)
13 Flushing ***** – Wimbledon of the US (6)
15 Full-back Ferrer or a hall for indoor tennis, perhaps (6)
17 Mother and I love it at Royal Ascot (5)
18 Country links Rusedski & Lewis (6)
21 Sachin Tendulkar, for example (6)
22 Vulnerable bone for those playing contact sports (4)
23 Former French tennis favourite, Yannik (4)
24 Most successful Rugby League player, now top coach (6)

CLUES DOWN:

1   Little fella with a big heart on the golf circuit (7)
2   McCrae, the rally driving ace (5)
3   ***** mid-off – sounds a stupid place to stand in cricket (5)
4   1990 World Cup Final was held here (4)
6   Doesn't make his team's starting line-up (7)
7   Derby's basketball team are no wash-outs (5)
11 Famous golfing venue in Scotland (5)
12 Try-scoring genius from France was the best ...(5)
14 Home of NFL and NBA (7)
16 Every team should have one (7)
17 Giant Irish striker popular with football fans from Sunderland (5)
18 Major sporting sponsors who love a sure-shot (5)
19 Bill, former opening batsman for England (5)
20 South African football star who has 'scaled' the heights (4)

COMING UP NEXT:

CARL FOGARTY FEATURE +
SKY SPORTS CALENDAR

CHECK OUT THE DATES
THAT MATTER IN OUR
MONTH-BY-MONTH GUIDE

SKY SPORTS 83

CARL FOGARTY

The MAN ... and his MACHINE !

A FEW THINGS YOU SHOULD KNOW ABOUT SUPERBIKES

★ Superbike racing began as a form of production racing where the race bikes, whilst highly tuned, at least resembled road bikes.

★ In 1988 ex-racer Steve McLaughlin and a team of businessmen decided to make the class into a world series to rival the Grand Prix.

★ To take part, each factory must build 200 of the bikes they wish to race and make them available for general sale. Most tend to go to other race teams or collectors.

★ Unlike GP bikes, superbikes are powered by four-stroke engines and cost about a million dollars (£630,000)

★ Superbike racing is getting bigger all the time and last season more than 80,000 people flocked to Brands Hatch for the European round.

★ The sport claimed its first fatality in 1995 when Japanese star Yasutomo Nagai died from multiple injuries days after crashing at Assen.

★ So far, only Honda and Ducati have taken the title with Foggy winning the World Championship three times on the Italian machine.

THE MACHINE:

ENGINE: 90° V-twin four stroke – Liquid cooled
CAPACITY: 996cc
BORE x STROKE: 98mm x 66mm
TIMING SYSTEM: DOHC, 4 valves per cylinder
FUEL SYSTEM: Electronic ignition
INJECTION IGNITION: Magneti Marelli
FINAL DRIVE: Regina chain
BRAKE HORSEPOWER: 163 HP at 11,500 rpm
TOP SPEED: 300km/h
TRANSMISSION:
Gearbox: 6-speed;
Clutch: dry, hydraulic control
CYCLE PARTS:
Frame: Steel trestle;
Front suspension: Ohlins upside-down fork;
Rear suspension: Magnesium swingarm, Ohlins single shock;
Front brakes: Brembo 2 x Ø320/290 rotors, Brembo 4 – piston calipers;
Rear brakes: Brembo 1 x Ø200 rotor, Brembo 2-pistons caliper
TYRES: Michelin
BIKE DIMENSIONS:
Length: 2030mm;
Width: 685mm;
Wheelbase: 1430mm;
Dry weight: 162kg;
Fuel tank capacity: 24 litres

They don't call him 'The Blackburn Bullet' for nothing. Carl Fogarty is one of the fastest men on two wheels and he has a cult following which would turn the majority of top sportsmen green with envy. But it's not just in Britain that 'Foggy' is an idol to so many would-be Superbike sensations; he's one of the most popular sports stars in Italy too! According to a survey of Italian sports fans, Fogarty is bigger news than any of the country's leading footballers and is up there in the national popularity stakes with Ferrari's Michael Schumacher and Italy's own Max Biaggi, Yamaha's Grand Prix pin-up. Not bad for a scruffy kid from the North West of England whose first foray into motorcycling was on the motorcross track.

He was pretty good too, but not good enough for his own liking so he quit. His attitude at the time was 'I'm never going to be world champion at this, so I'll try something else'. And he did; taking part in his first road race in 1984 – on a 600cc F2 Ducati. The rest, as they say, is history and now 15 years on he's a living legend in the exhilarating world of superbikes.

He did his reputation in Italy no harm whatsoever when he won both races in front of 65,000 adoring fans at Monza in May to go no fewer than 55 points clear at the top of the World Superbike Championship table. His 53rd career win delighted the crowd – not to mention his Bologna-based Ducati employers – and set him up nicely for a fourth world title in six years.

Afterwards, he tried to convince everyone that he would love to quit the sport but he added: "Although I want to retire I can't until these guys beat me. And they can't beat me yet." Not arrogance, sheer confidence in his riding ability, not to mention the power and handling of his Ducati; man and machine in perfect harmony. One of the 'guys' he was talking about was the American Colin Edwards whose Honda was initially adjudged to have crossed the line a fraction of a second ahead of Foggy at Monza. But, in a bizarre double twist, the race was then declared a draw before first place was finally and dramatically awarded to the Ducati man by FIVE THOUSANDTHS OF A SECOND!

"To win by that sort of margin is not just close; it's amazing, but I've lost by that margin before," declared Fogarty whose laid back attitude in this high-octane sport is equally incredible. "I'm more relaxed about this season than ever before," he confirmed. "Winning is what motivates me. I don't even like riding motorbikes and never ride one on the road. I just love to race and win."

And what about his popularity with the Italian sporting public? "I'm a bit surprised I was voted third in that poll. I thought I'd have won it easily," he joked in his typical casual manner.

But Ducati spokesman Michele Monsetti was deadly serious when he said: "Carl is a major star in Italy. Everyone knows his face as he is pictured on the cover of magazines all the time. People see him as a normal guy, unlike some sportsmen, and fans know he is one of them." A normal guy who just happens to be the best in the world at what he does ...

THE FOGGY FACTS

Year	Title	Pos
1988	World Formula 1 Championship (Honda)	1st
1989	World Formula 1 Championship (Honda)	1st
1990	FIM Formula 1 World Cup (Honda)	1st
1991	World Superbike Championship (Honda)	7th
1992	World Endurance Championship (Kawasaki)	1st
	World Superbike Championship (Ducati)	9th
1993	World Superbike Championship (Ducati)	2nd
1994	World Superbike Championship (Ducati)	1st
1995	World Superbike Championship (Ducati)	1st
1996	World Superbike Championship (Honda)	4th
1997	World Superbike Championship (Ducati)	2nd
1998	World Superbike Championship (Ducati)	1st

At the time of this annual going to press, Fogarty was well on course to retain his Superbike title in 1999.

WE'VE GOT ALL THE ANSWERS!

SKYSPORTS SUPERBRAIN (Pages 14-15):

CRYPTIC QUIZ: 1 'Rocket' Ronnie O'Sullivan; 2 Dennis Wise; 3 John Crawley; 4 Tim Henman; 5 Leeds Rhinos.
UGLY MUGS: 1 Anna Kournikova 2 Lennox Lewis 3 David Batty
MISSING LINK: 1 Ernie ELS; 2 Dwight YORKE; 3 Andy GRAY; 4 Suarav GANGULY; 5 Mike CATT.
ALL SHOOK UP: 1 Greg Rusedski; 2 Carl Fogarty; 3 Jeremy Guscott; 4 Dwight Yorke; 5 Henry Paul.
ANDY'S BRAIN TEASERS: 1 Seve Ballesteros; 2 318; 3 Jonathon Woodgate.

WORDSEARCH: Wembley, Roland Garros, Ascot, Lords, Belfry, Augusta, Twickenham, Trent Bridge, Nou Camp, Monte Carlo.

W	A	D	B	N	O	U	C	A	M	P	R
T	E	O	C	H	G	I	Q	R	O	V	O
R	Y	M	X	G	N	J	X	S	N	U	L
E	A	A	B	R	O	A	C	C	T	E	A
N	B	H	W	L	P	K	A	Y	E	A	N
T	O	C	S	A	E	L	N	F	C	D	D
B	B	E	L	F	R	Y	A	I	A	T	G
R	G	K	K	A	S	G	R	G	R	I	A
I	H	C	J	N	R	M	I	H	L	G	R
D	H	A	U	G	U	S	T	A	O	E	R
G	T	W	I	C	K	E	N	H	A	M	O
E	B	T	I	R	P	O	L	O	R	D	S

SKYSPORTS SUPERBRAIN (Pages 78-79)

CRYPTIC QUIZ: 1 Andy Cole; 2 Austin Healey; 3 Richard Branson; 4 Nick Knight; 5 Justin Rose.UGLY MUGS: 1 Marcus Buckland 2 David Gower 3 Rob McCaffrey
MISSING LINK: 1 Jimmy WHITE; 2 Steve WAUGH; 3 Tony ADAMS; 4 Ian DARKE; 5 Greg NORMAN.
ALL SHOOK UP: Shane Warne; 2 Martina Hingis; 3 Lennox Lewis; 4 Greg Norman; 5 Alan Shearer.
ANDY'S BRAIN TEASERS: 1 Halifax; 2 Martin Johnson; 3 Alan Shearer.

WORDSEARCH: Wimbledon, World Cup, Grand Prix, FA Cup, Tour De France, The Derby, The Open, Olympics, The Ashes, Milk Race.

G	W	I	M	B	L	E	D	O	N	P	T
R	E	O	C	H	G	I	Q	R	O	O	O
A	Y	M	X	G	N	J	X	S	U	L	L
N	E	P	T	H	E	D	E	R	B	Y	M
D	M	H	W	L	P	K	D	Y	S	M	N
P	I	C	S	A	E	E	N	E	C	P	D
R	L	E	L	F	F	Y	H	I	A	I	G
I	K	K	K	R	S	S	R	G	R	C	F
X	R	C	A	N	A	M	I	H	L	S	A
D	A	N	N	E	P	O	E	H	T	E	C
C	C	W	H	R	O	R	S	I	L	R	U
E	E	T	I	W	O	R	L	D	C	U	P

Crossword page 32:

E		C		S				M		T		S
D		O	C	H	E		D	U	R	H	A	M
W		L		A		M		L		R		A
A	T	L	A	N	T	A		L	E	E	D	S
R		I		E		R		A		E		H
D	I	N	O		S	K	I	L	L			
S		S		D		J		Y		F		R
			D	U	V	A	L		L	O	V	E
S		S		N		M		E		G		A
P	I	T	C	H		E	N	G	L	A	N	D
I		U		I		S		Y		R		I
K	U	M	B	L	E		S	P	O	T		N
E		P		L				T		Y		G

Crossword page 84:

W		C	O	R	S	E	R		A	R	M	S
O		O			I		O			E		T
O	L	L	Y		L	E	M	A	N	S		O
S		I			L		E			E		R
N	I	N	E	T	Y			S	C	R	U	M
A				H				E		V		
M	E	A	D	O	W		A	L	B	E	R	T
		M		R				L				R
Q	U	E	E	N			C	A	N	A	D	A
U		R			F		A			T		I
I		I	N	D	I	A	N		S	H	I	N
N		C			S		O			E		E
N	O	A	H		H	A	N	L	E	Y		R

	MON	TUE	WED	THU	FRI	SAT	SUN
JANUARY						1	2
	3	4	5	6	7	8	9
	10	11	12	13	14	15	16
	17	18	19	20	21	22	23
	24	25	26	27	28	29	30
	31						

SPORTING LEGENDS

EUSÉBIO
(Eusébio da Silva Ferreira)

PORTUGAL'S WORLD CUP SUPERSTAR

Born: Lourenço Marques, Mozambique, January 25, 1942

THE GREATEST PORTUGUESE PLAYER OF ALL TIME WAS, IN FACT, BORN AND RAISED IN MOZAMBIQUE, WHICH WAS THEN A PORTUGESE EAST AFRICAN COLONY. *EUSÉBIO* BURST ONTO THE WORLD SCENE AT THE AGE OF 19, WHEN *BENFICA* PLAYED *SANTOS* OF *BRAZIL* IN A TOURNAMENT IN FRANCE. HE ONLY PLAYED IN THE SECOND-HALF, BUT HIS SENSATIONAL HAT-TRICK PUSHED THE GREAT *PELÉ* OUT OF THE SPOTLIGHT. IN THE AUTUMN OF 1961, AFTER JUST 25 APPEARANCES FOR *BENFICA*, HE MADE HIS DEBUT FOR *PORTUGAL*, GOING ON TO SCORE 41 GOALS IN 64 INTERNATIONALS. THE FOLLOWING YEAR, HE SCORED TWICE IN *BENFICA'S* 5-3 EUROPEAN CUP FINAL VICTORY OVER *REAL MADRID* (HE GAINED RUNNERS-UP MEDALS IN 1963, 1965 AND 1968.) THE 1965 EUROPEAN FOOTBALLER OF THE YEAR, HE WAS MAGNIFICENT IN THE 1966 WORLD CUP FINALS, HIS NINE GOALS – INCLUDING FOUR AGAINST *NORTH KOREA* IN ONE OF THE GREATEST COMEBACKS IN THE HISTORY OF THE GAME – MAKING HIM TOURNAMENT TOP-SCORER AND HELPING *PORTUGAL* TO THIRD PLACE. A MAJESTIC STRIKER, ADMIRED FOR HIS SKILLS AND HIS LEGENDARY SPORTSMANSHIP, HE SCORED 316 GOALS FOR *BENFICA* IN 294 LEAGUE GAMES, BEFORE FINISHING HIS CAREER IN NORTH AMERICA WITH SPELLS IN BOSTON, TORONTO AND LAS VEGAS.

JANUARY

DAVID GINOLA
Born January 25, 1967

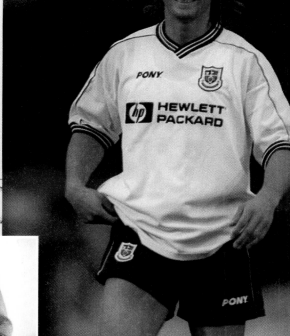

On January 1, 1989 ERIC BRISTOW became the first darts player to receive the MBE ...

Russian weightlifter VASILY ALEKSEYEV was born on January 7, 1942. He set 80 world records in seven years ...

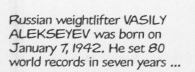

FRANK LEBOEUF
Born January 22, 1968

Boxing legend MUHAMMAD ALI was born CASSIUS CLAY on January 17, 1942

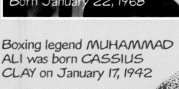

BRAZIL'S World Cup '94 hero ROMARIO was born January 29, 1966

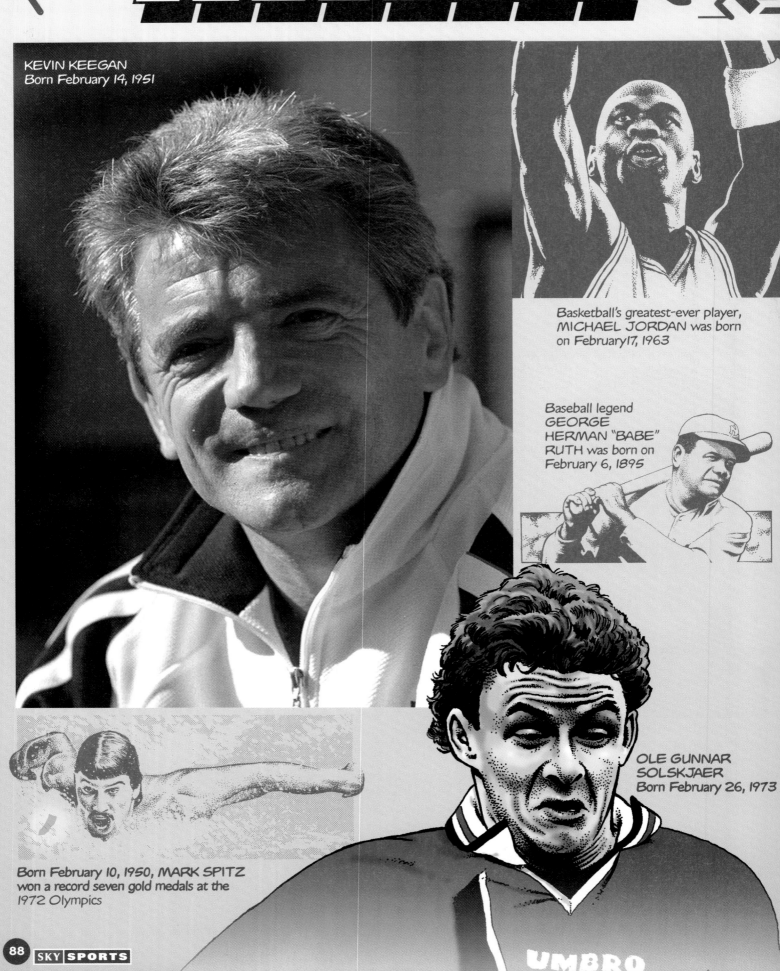

FEBRUARY

KEVIN KEEGAN
Born February 14, 1951

Basketball's greatest-ever player, MICHAEL JORDAN was born on February 17, 1963

Baseball legend GEORGE HERMAN "BABE" RUTH was born on February 6, 1895

OLE GUNNAR SOLSKJAER
Born February 26, 1973

Born February 10, 1950, MARK SPITZ won a record seven gold medals at the 1972 Olympics

UMBRO

MON	TUE	WED	THU	FRI	SAT	SUN
	1	2	3	4	5	6
7	8	9	10	11	12	13
14	15	16	17	18	19	20
21	22	23	24	25	26	27
28	29					

FEBRUARY

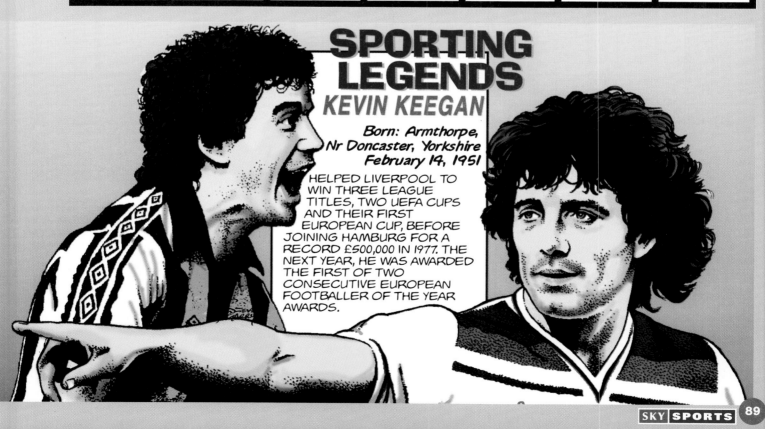

SPORTING LEGENDS
KEVIN KEEGAN

Born: Armthorpe, Nr Doncaster, Yorkshire February 14, 1951

HELPED LIVERPOOL TO WIN THREE LEAGUE TITLES, TWO UEFA CUPS AND THEIR FIRST EUROPEAN CUP, BEFORE JOINING HAMBURG FOR A RECORD £500,000 IN 1977. THE NEXT YEAR, HE WAS AWARDED THE FIRST OF TWO CONSECUTIVE EUROPEAN FOOTBALLER OF THE YEAR AWARDS.

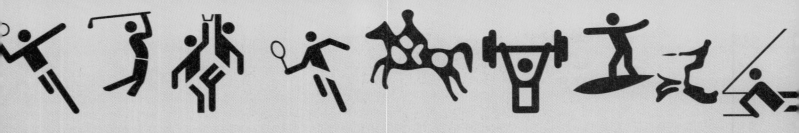

		MON	TUE	WED	THU	FRI	SAT	SUN

MON	TUE	WED	THU	FRI	SAT	SUN
		1	2	3	4	5
6	7	8	9	10	11	12
13	14	15	16	17	18	19
20	21	22	23	24	25	26
27	28	29	30	31		

MARCH

LOTHAR MATTHÄUS

*Born: Erlangen,
March 21, 1961*

FORMER EUROPEAN
FOOTBALLER OF THE YEAR,
WHO HAS WON THE WORLD
CUP AND THE EUROPEAN
CHAMPIONSHIP WITH
GERMANY AND EARNED
OVER A CENTURY OF CAPS.

SPORTING LEGENDS

MARCH

PAUL MERSON
Born March 20, 1968

JOE CALZAGHE
Born March 23, 1972

Globetrotting US international footballer ROY WEGERLE was born in South Africa on March 19, 1964

JESSE OWENS, the track star whose four gold medals at the 1936 Berlin Olympics so infuriated ADOLF HITLER, died on March 31, 1980

APRIL

On April 20, 1981, STEVE DAVIS won the World Professional Snooker title for the first time

TEDDY SHERINGHAM
Born April 2, 1966

DAVID GOWER
Born April 1, 1957

SACHIN TENDULKAR
Born April 24, 1973

MON	TUE	WED	THU	FRI	SAT	SUN
					1	2
3	4	5	6	7	8	9
10	11	12	13	14	15	16
17	18	19	20	21	22	23
24	25	26	27	28	29	30

APRIL

SPORTING LEGENDS

BOBBY MOORE

CAPTAIN OF ENGLAND'S WORLD CUP WINNING SIDE

Born: Barking, April 17, 1941
14 World Cup appearances

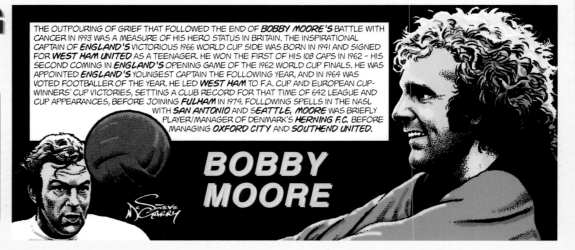

THE OUTPOURING OF GRIEF THAT FOLLOWED THE END OF *BOBBY MOORE'S* BATTLE WITH CANCER IN 1993 WAS A MEASURE OF HIS HERO STATUS IN BRITAIN. THE INSPIRATIONAL CAPTAIN OF *ENGLAND'S* VICTORIOUS 1966 WORLD CUP SIDE WAS BORN IN 1941 AND SIGNED FOR *WEST HAM UNITED* AS A TEENAGER. HE WON THE FIRST OF HIS 108 CAPS IN 1962 – HIS SECOND COMING IN *ENGLAND'S* OPENING GAME OF THE 1962 WORLD CUP FINALS. HE WAS APPOINTED *ENGLAND'S* YOUNGEST CAPTAIN THE FOLLOWING YEAR, AND IN 1964 WAS VOTED FOOTBALLER OF THE YEAR. HE LED *WEST HAM* TO F.A. CUP AND EUROPEAN CUP-WINNERS' CUP VICTORIES, SETTING A CLUB RECORD FOR THAT TIME OF 642 LEAGUE AND CUP APPEARANCES, BEFORE JOINING *FULHAM* IN 1974. FOLLOWING SPELLS IN THE NASL WITH *SAN ANTONIO* AND *SEATTLE, MOORE* WAS BRIEFLY PLAYER/MANAGER OF DENMARK'S *HERNING F.C.* BEFORE MANAGING *OXFORD CITY* AND *SOUTHEND UNITED*.

BOBBY MOORE

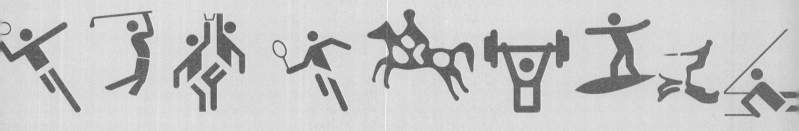

MON	TUE	WED	THU	FRI	SAT	SUN
1	2	3	4	5	6	7
8	9	10	11	12	13	14
15	16	17	18	19	20	21
22	23	24	25	26	27	28
29	30	31				

MAY

SPORTING LEGENDS

FRANCO BARESI

LEGENDARY
ITALIAN
DEFENDER

Born: Travagliato, May 8, 1960
10 World Cup appearances

FRANCO BARESI WAS BORN IN TRAVAGLIATO IN 1960 AND MADE HIS SERIE A DEBUT FOR **AC MILAN** TWO WEEKS BEFORE HIS 18TH BIRTHDAY. FOR MUCH OF HIS EARLY INTERNATIONAL CAREER, HE LIVED IN THE SHADOW OF LEGENDARY **JUVENTUS** SWEEPER **GAETANO SCIREA** – **BARESI** WAS A NON-PLAYING MEMBER OF **ITALY'S** 1982 WORLD CUP SQUAD AND WAS OMITTED COMPLETELY FROM THE 1986 LINE-UP – BUT HIS FORTUNES CHANGED IN THE MID-1980S. HE BECAME A KEY FIGURE IN THE NATIONAL TEAM AND THE FOUNDATION STONE ON WHICH **ARRIGO SACCHI** BUILT HIS ALL-CONQUERING **MILAN** SIDE. **BARESI'S** PERFORMANCES AT THE 1988 EUROPEAN CHAMPIONSHIPS AND **ITALIA '90** ESTABLISHED HIM AS ONE OF THE BEST SWEEPERS IN THE WORLD, BUT FOLLOWING **ITALY'S** FAILURE TO QUALIFY FOR THE 1992 EUROPEAN CHAMPIONSHIPS, **BARESI** RETIRED FROM THE INTERNATIONAL GAME. HOWEVER, HE WAS PERSUADED TO RETURN TO THE FOLD FOR THE 1994 WORLD CUP AND CAPTAINED **ITALY** TO THE FINAL, WHERE A PENALTY SHOOT-OUT DENIED HIM A WINNER'S MEDAL.

MAY

CLIVE ALLEN
Born May 20, 1961

ROCKY GRAZIANO, whose "SOMEBODY UP THERE LIKES ME" autobiography was filmed with PAUL NEWMAN in the lead role, died on May 22, 1990

DAVID BECKHAM
Born May 2, 1975

West Indian batting superstar BRIAN LARA was born on May 2, 1969

JUNE

COLIN MONTGOMERIE
Born June 23, 1963

On June 16, 1982 BRYAN ROBSON scored the fastest goal in World Cup history, just 27 seconds into the ENGLAND v FRANCE clash. ROBSON added another later in the game as ENGLAND ran out 3-1 winners

June 2, 1954 – LESTER PIGGOTT rode the first of his nine Derby winners

MON	TUE	WED	THU	FRI	SAT	SUN
			1	2	3	4
5	6	7	8	9	10	11
12	13	14	15	16	17	18
19	20	21	22	23	24	25
26	27	28	29	30		

JUNE

SPORTING LEGENDS

MICHEL PLATINI

CAPTAINED
FRANCE TO
EURO GLORY

*Born: Jouef, June 21, 1955
14 World Cup appearances
5 goals*

MICHEL PLATINI MADE HIS DEBUT ON THE WORLD STAGE AT THE 1976 OLYMPICS IN MONTREAL, AND TWO YEARS LATER, WAS IMPRESSIVE IN A FRANCE SIDE THAT WAS DESPERATELY UNLUCKY TO EXIT EARLY FROM THE WORLD CUP TOURNAMENT. IN 1982, PLATINI INSPIRED FRANCE TO FOURTH PLACE IN THE WORLD CUP AND IN 1984, CAPTAINED HIS COUNTRY TO VICTORY IN THE EUROPEAN CHAMPIONSHIPS. TWO YEARS LATER, PLATINI'S FRANCE WERE ONCE MORE ELIMINATED IN A WORLD CUP SEMI-FINAL BY WEST GERMANY. THE FIRST PLAYER TO WIN THREE SUCCESSIVE EUROPEAN FOOTBALLER OF THE YEAR AWARDS, PLATINI WON DOMESTIC HONOURS WITH NANCY AND ST. ETIENNE, BEFORE JOINING ITALY'S JUVENTUS, WITH WHOM HE WON THE EUROPEAN CUP AND CUP-WINNERS' CUP. THREE TIMES TOP ITALIAN LEAGUE GOALSCORER, HE RETIRED IN 1987, HAVING SCORED 348 GOALS IN 648 PROFESSIONAL GAMES. IN 1988, HE WAS PERSUADED TO TAKE OVER AS FRANCE'S COACH AND HE STEERED HIS COUNTRY TO THE 1992 EUROPEAN CHAMPIONSHIPS. CAPPED 72 TIMES – 50 AS CAPTAIN – HE SCORED 41 GOALS FOR HIS COUNTRY.

MON	TUE	WED	THU	FRI	SAT	SUN
					1	2
3	4	5	6	7	8	9
10	11	12	13	14	15	16
17	18	19	20	21	22	23
24	25	26	27	28	29	30
31						

JULY

SPORTING LEGENDS

MARIO KEMPES

"EL MATADOR" –
ARGENTINA'S 1978
WORLD CUP HERO

Born: Belville, Córdoba, July 15, 1954
18 World Cup appearances
6 goals

"*EL MATADOR*" BEGAN HIS CAREER WITH *INSTITUTO CORDOBA*, MOVING TO ROSARIO CENTRAL SHORTLY BEFORE HE MADE HIS INTERNATIONAL DEBUT IN 1973. THREE YEARS LATER HE JOINED SPAIN'S *VALENCIA*, TOPPING THE LEAGUE'S GOALSCORING CHART IN HIS FIRST TWO FULL SEASONS FOR THE CLUB. HE WAS THE ONLY EUROPEAN-BASED PLAYER CALLED UP FOR *ARGENTINA'S* 1978 WORLD CUP SQUAD AND HE REPAID COACH *CESAR LUIS MENOTTI'S* FAITH BY SCORING SIX GOALS, INCLUDING TWO IN THE FINAL IN THE VICTORY OVER *HOLLAND*. HE GAINED A EUROPEAN CUP-WINNERS' CUP MEDAL WITH *VALENCIA* IN 1980, BEFORE RETURNING TO ARGENTINA WITH *RIVER PLATE* IN 1981. IN 1984, HE TURNED OUT IN A SERIES OF FRIENDLIES FOR *TOTTENHAM HOTSPUR* BEFORE REJOINING *VALENCIA*. HIS TRAVELS TOOK HIM ON TO *HERCULES* IN SPAIN, BEFORE WINDING DOWN HIS PLAYING CAREER IN AUSTRIA. HE LATER COACHED ALBANIAN SIDE *LUSHNJE*, BUT WAS FORCED TO FLEE THE COUNTRY WITH THE OUTBREAK OF CIVIL UNREST IN 1996.

JULY

MARTIN KEOWN
Born July 24, 1966

July 23, 1989,
GREG LeMOND
won the TOUR de
FRANCE for the
second time

GIANLUCA VIALLI
Born July 9, 1964

AUGUST

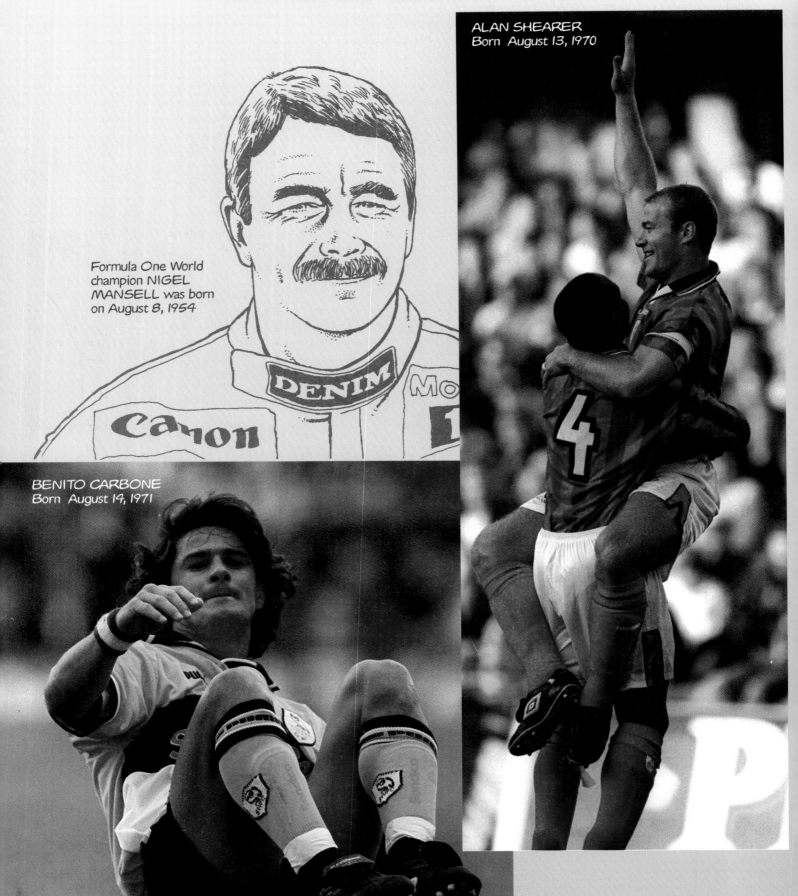

Formula One World champion NIGEL MANSELL was born on August 8, 1954

ALAN SHEARER
Born August 13, 1970

BENITO CARBONE
Born August 14, 1971

	MON	TUE	WED	THU	FRI	SAT	SUN
		1	2	3	4	5	6
	7	8	9	10	11	12	13
AUGUST	14	15	16	17	18	19	20
	21	22	23	24	25	26	27
	28	29	30	31			

ALAN SHEARER

Born: Newcastle, August 13, 1970

STARTED HIS CAREER AT **SOUTHAMPTON**, BEFORE JOINING **BLACKBURN ROVERS** IN 1992 FOR £3.6 MILLION. WON THE LEAGUE TITLE WITH **ROVERS** IN 1995 AND JOINED **NEWCASTLE UNITED** THE FOLLOWING YEAR FOR A WORLD-RECORD £15 MILLION.

SPORTING LEGENDS

	MON	TUE	WED	THU	FRI	SAT	SUN
S E P T E M B E R					1	2	3
	4	5	6	7	8	9	10
	11	12	13	14	15	16	17
	18	19	20	21	22	23	24
	25	26	27	28	29	30	

SPORTING LEGENDS

FRANZ BECKENBAUER

 **"DER KAISER"**

Born: Munich, September 11, 1945
18 World Cup appearances
5 goals

BECKENBAUER WON THE FIRST OF HIS 103 CAPS AT THE AGE OF 19, AFTER JUST 27 SENIOR GAMES FOR **BAYERN MUNICH**. BORN IN MUNICH IN 1945, HIS ELEGANT MIDFIELD PLAY AND FOUR GOALS HELPED **WEST GERMANY** REACH THE 1966 WORLD CUP FINAL, BUT HIS MAN-MARKING ROLE ON **ENGLAND'S BOBBY CHARLTON** DEPRIVED THE TEAM OF HIS CREATIVITY AND PERHAPS COST THEM VICTORY. A LOSING SEMI-FINALIST IN 1970, HE CAPTAINED HIS COUNTRY TO WORLD CUP GLORY IN 1974, HAVING PERFECTED THE ROLE OF ATTACKING SWEEPER. TWO YEARS EARLIER, HE HAD LED **WEST GERMANY** TO VICTORY IN THE EUROPEAN CHAMPIONSHIPS. TWICE EUROPEAN FOOTBALLER OF THE YEAR, HIS CAREER WITH **BAYERN MUNICH** YIELDED FOUR LEAGUE TITLES, FOUR WEST GERMAN CUPS, THREE EUROPEAN CUPS AND THE CUP-WINNERS' CUP. HE LATER HELPED THE **NEW YORK COSMOS** WIN TWO NASL TITLES, BEFORE RETURNING TO GERMANY TO CAPTURE THE 1982 LEAGUE CROWN WITH **HAMBURG**. APPOINTED NATIONAL COACH IN 1984, "**KAISER FRANZ**" BOWED OUT IN GLORY AFTER STEERING **GERMANY** TO 1990 WORLD CUP TRIUMPH.

SEPTEMBER

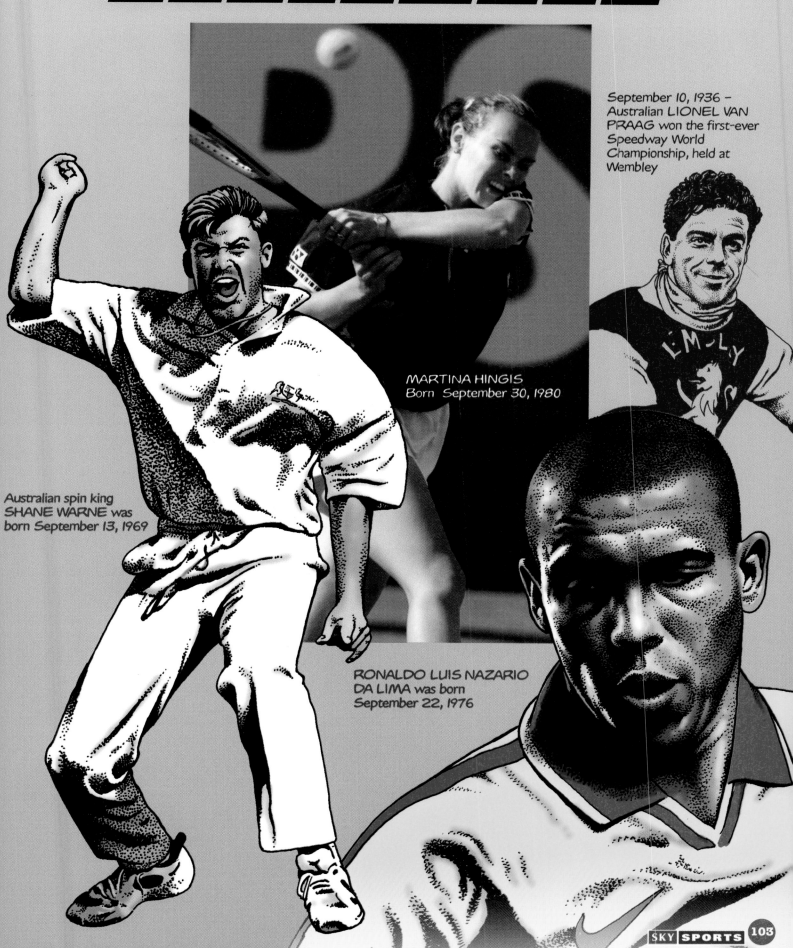

September 10, 1936 – Australian LIONEL VAN PRAAG won the first-ever Speedway World Championship, held at Wembley

MARTINA HINGIS
Born September 30, 1980

Australian spin king SHANE WARNE was born September 13, 1969

RONALDO LUIS NAZARIO DA LIMA was born September 22, 1976

OCTOBER

ANDY COLE
Born October 15, 1971

Superbowl winning
quarterback STEVE
YOUNG was born on
October 11, 1961

GRAEME Le SAUX
Born October 17, 1968

TOMMY "THE HIT MAN" HEARNS
Born October 18, 1958

	MON	TUE	WED	THU	FRI	SAT	SUN
							1
	2	3	4	5	6	7	8
	9	10	11	12	13	14	15
	16	17	18	19	20	21	22
	23	24	25	26	27	28	29
	30	31					

OCTOBER

SPORTING LEGENDS

PELÉ

THE LIVING LEGEND

Born: Tres Corações, Minas Gerais, October 23, 1940
14 World Cup appearances
12 goals

EDSON ARANTES DO NASCIMENTO WAS BORN IN TRES CORAÇÕES, MINAS GERAIS, BRAZIL ON OCTOBER 23, 1940. KNOWN TO THE WORLD AS **PELÉ**, BY THE TIME HE FINALLY RETIRED IN 1977, HE HAD BECOME THE MOST FAMOUS SOCCER PLAYER ON EARTH! HE MADE HIS INTERNATIONAL DEBUT AT 16 AND WENT ON TO SCORE 97 GOALS IN 111 GAMES FOR **BRAZIL**, INCLUDING A DOZEN IN THE FOUR WORLD CUP TOURNAMENTS THAT EARNED HIM THREE WINNER'S MEDALS. **PELÉ** WAS 15 WHEN HE SCORED ON HIS DEBUT FOR **SANTOS** - 14 YEARS AND 1254 GAMES LATER HE RETIRED FOR THE FIRST TIME, HAVING SCORED 1216 GOALS. IN 1975, **NEW YORK COSMOS** TEMPTED HIM BACK INTO THE SPORT WITH A $4.5 MILLION CONTRACT. HE TOOK HIS CAREER TALLY TO A TOTAL OF 1283 GOALS AS HE ALMOST SINGLE-HANDEDLY LAUNCHED SOCCER IN THE U.S.A.

MON	TUE	WED	THU	FRI	SAT	SUN
		1	2	3	4	5
6	7	8	9	10	11	12
13	14	15	16	17	18	19
20	21	22	23	24	25	26
27	28	29	30			

NOVEMBER

SPORTING LEGENDS

GARY LINEKER

 ENGLAND'S MASTER POACHER

Born: Leicester, November 30, 1960
12 World Cup appearances
10 goals

GARY LINEKER BEGAN HIS CAREER WITH **LEICESTER CITY**, SCORING 26 GOALS IN THE 1982/83 SEASON THEY WON PROMOTION TO THE TOP FLIGHT. HE JOINED LEAGUE CHAMPIONS **EVERTON** IN 1985 AND SCORED 30 GOALS TO TOP THE LEAGUE'S GOALSCORING CHARTS. HE MADE HISTORY IN THE 1986 WORLD CUP IN MEXICO, WHEN HE BECAME THE FIRST BRITISH PLAYER TO TOP-SCORE IN THE TOURNAMENT, HIS SIX GOALS CATAPULTING HIM TO WORLD SUPERSTARDOM AND EARNING HIM A TRANSFER TO **BARCELONA**, WITH WHOM HE WON THE EUROPEAN CUP-WINNERS CUP IN 1989. RETURNING TO ENGLAND WITH **TOTTENHAM HOTSPUR**, HE SCORED FOUR OF **ENGLAND'S** GOALS AT **ITALIA '90**. HAVING NARROWLY MISSED **BOBBY CHARLTON'S ENGLAND** SCORING RECORD, **LINEKER** RETIRED FROM INTERNATIONAL SOCCER AND TOOK UP A LUCRATIVE CONTRACT IN JAPAN WITH **GRAMPUS EIGHT OF NAGOYA**.

NOVEMBER

ANDY GRAY
Born November
30, 1955

Baseball great JOE
DiMAGGIO was
born on November
25, 1914

Depressed after
the death of his
wife in childbirth
two years
earlier, 29-year
-old former
Champion jockey
FRED ARCHER
committed suicide
on November 4,
1886

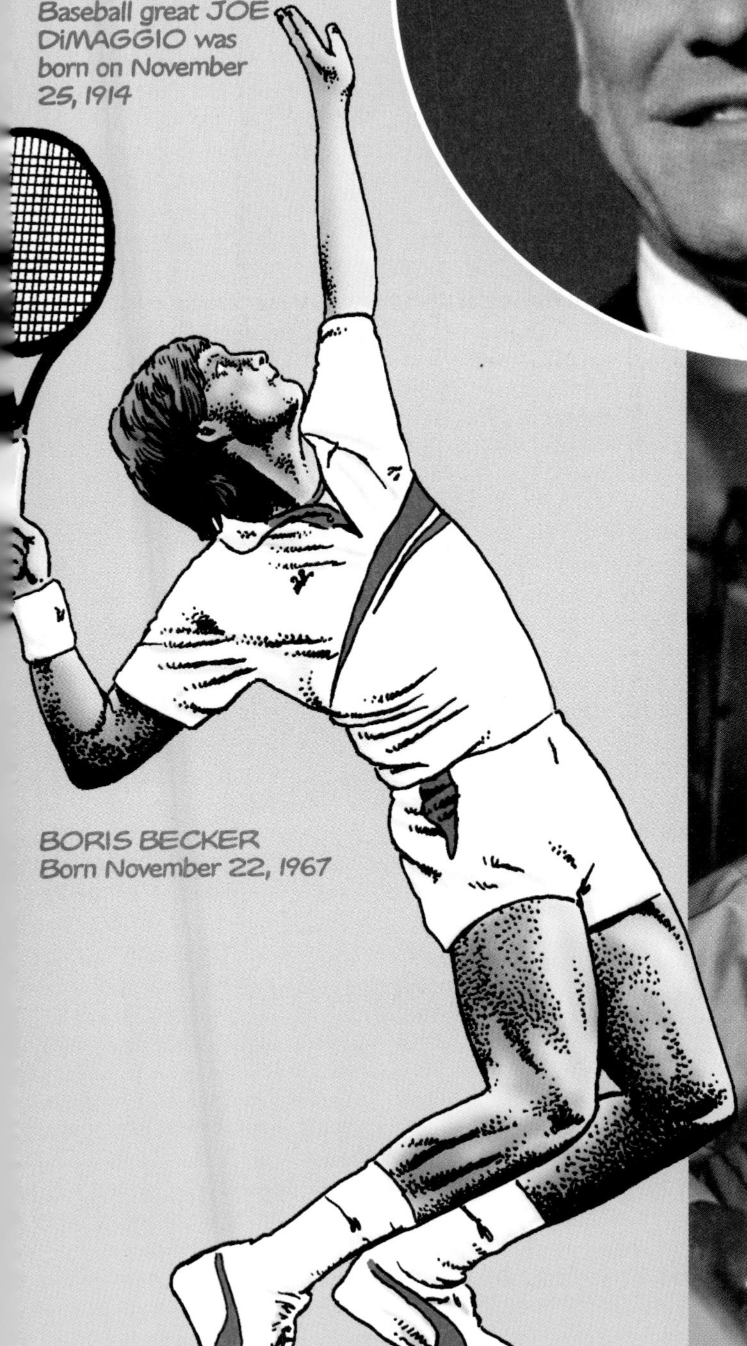

BORIS BECKER
Born November 22, 1967

IAN BOTHAM
Born November 24, 1955

DECEMBER

Olympic gold-winning skater KATARINA WITT was born on December 3, 1965

TIGER WOODS Born December 30, 1975

MICHAEL OWEN Born December 14, 1979

DAVID BATTY Born December 2, 1968

MON	TUE	WED	THU	FRI	SAT	SUN
				1	2	3
4	5	6	7	8	9	10
11	12	13	14	15	16	17
18	19	20	21	22	23	24
25	26	27	28	29	30	31

DECEMBER

SPORTING LEGENDS

GORDON BANKS

"BANKS OF ENGLAND"

Born: Sheffield, December 30, 1937
9 World Cup appearances
6 clean sheets

GORDON BANKS PLAYED ONE SEASON IN THE ENGLISH THIRD DIVISION WITH **CHESTERFIELD** BEFORE MOVING INTO THE TOP FLIGHT WITH **LEICESTER CITY** IN 1959. EIGHT YEARS LATER, HE JOINED **STOKE CITY**. HE WON THE FIRST OF HIS 73 CAPS IN 1963 AND WAS OUTSTANDING IN **ENGLAND'S** VICTORIOUS 1966 WORLD CUP CAMPAIGN - HE DIDN'T CONCEDE A GOAL UNTIL THE SEMI-FINAL! FOUR YEARS LATER, WHEN **ENGLAND** DEFENDED THE TITLE IN MEXICO, **BANKS** PULLED OFF ONE OF THE MOST FAMOUS REACTION SAVES IN HISTORY, TURNING A POINT-BLANK **PELÉ** HEADER AWAY FOR A CORNER. A MYSTERY STOMACH AILMENT RULED **BANKS** OUT OF THE QUARTER-FINAL, AND IN HIS ABSENCE **ENGLAND** SQUANDERED A 2-0 LEAD TO ALLOW **WEST GERMANY** A FAMOUS COMEBACK VICTORY. IN 1972, HE HELPED **STOKE CITY** TO WIN THE LEAGUE CUP - THE FIRST TROPHY IN THE CLUB'S HISTORY - AND WAS VOTED FOOTBALLER OF THE YEAR. LATER THAT SAME YEAR, TRAGEDY STRUCK WHEN **BANKS** LOST AN EYE IN A CAR CRASH AND HIS CAREER AT THE HIGHEST LEVEL WAS OVER.